Enjoy the read!
Perspective for real life!

~Barb Rawalt

Andrea,

Enjoy the book! Christine

[signature]

BARBARA RAWALT

the parable of the fly

TRUE STRENGTH
FOR TOUGH TIMES

Copyright © 2023 by Barbara Rawalt

All rights reserved solely by the author. The author guarantees all contents are original and do not infringe upon the legal rights of any other person or work. No part of this book may be reproduced in any form without the permission of the author. The views expressed in this book are not necessarily those of the publisher.

First paperback edition July 2023

Unless otherwise indicated, all Scripture quotations are from the ESV® Bible (The Holy Bible, English Standard Version®), copyright © 2001 by Crossway, a publishing ministry of Good News Publishers. Used by permission. All rights reserved.

Scripture quotations marked NLT are taken from the Holy Bible, New Living Translation, copyright © 1996, 2004, 2015 by Tyndale House Foundation. Used by permission of Tyndale House Publishers, Carol Stream, Illinois 60188. All rights reserved.

Scripture quotations marked MSG are taken from The Message, copyright © 1993, 2002, 2018 by Eugene H. Peterson. Used by permission of NavPress. All rights reserved. Represented by Tyndale House Publishing.

Scripture quotations marked TPT are from The Passion Translation®. Copyright © 2017, 2018, 2020 by Passion & Fire Ministries, Inc. Used by permission. All rights reserved. ThePassionTranslation.com.

Cover design and author photo: Brett Rawalt

Printed in the United States of America by Gorham Printing, Centralia, WA.

ISBN: 978-1-7342896-9-5

DEDICATION

To the courage of my grandparents: Emil and Hilda, Karl Ivar and Anna — who left their lands to begin a new life in America. What bravery — thank you so much.

To the commitment of my parents: Bernie and Marge — both 1st-generation American-born, who raised my sisters and I in a loving and caring home. Thank you so very kindly!

To the love of my husband Mike, whose giving extends and continues to grow through these 56 years. Thank you so much!

To the joy of relationship with our sons: Brett and Christian, and daughter-in-law Suzi: what blessing through the years. You are such gifts to us. Thank you!

To the blessing of our many grandchildren: Hosanna, Molly, Micah and Kelly, Nisha, Max, Ben, Harry, Genevieve, and Ellie. May you strongly carry the torch of life in Jesus to your circles of influence and multiplied generations. Thank you!

To Jesus, my Source of true ongoing life. It seems so inadequate, but thank You, dear Jesus, thank You.

TABLE OF CONTENTS

Endorsements viii
Acknowledgments xi
Introduction xiii
Prelude: The Parable of the Fly xv
1. One Thing 1
2. Quiet Center 5
3. Towny Girl in the Woods 9
4. Change and the City 17
5. Do You Know Who You Are? 21
6. A Question 25
7. There is a River 29
8. Mudflats 33
9. Steady in Unsteady Times 37
10. Wear These Truths 41
11. Year of the Dance, Part 1 43
12. Year of the Dance, Part 2 47
13. Year of the Dance, Part 3 51
14. Onramps 55
15. Faithful God 61
16. Beloved: Story from a Vineyard, Part 1 65
17. Beloved: Story from a Vineyard, Part 2 69
18. The Pause 77
19. The Power of Small 81

20. Lemon Tree in the Marketplace 85
21. Geranium Wisdom 89
22. God and the Way Things Are 91
23. Prince of Peace............................. 93
24. Change the Atmosphere 95
25. Get the Boats Ready 99
26. Agent 99 and Chaos......................... 103
27. Receiving 107
28. Dichotomies................................ 111
29. Real News.................................. 113
30. At the Beach............................... 117
31. The Key of Peace 121
32. Principles of Refreshing 125
33. Orphan..................................... 129
34. Blaze Orange Dream 135
35. The Role of Joy 141
36. Sturdy Steady House and Life................ 145
37. Clutter 149
38. Beauty..................................... 151
39. God of Rainbows and Light Sabers 153
40. Don't Miss Dessert 155
41. World Book Dreams 161
42. Crossroads 165
Conclusion 169
Dear Reader 173
Appendix: Keys to True Strength 174

ENDORSEMENTS

"I have thoroughly enjoyed reading each section of this book, The Parable of the Fly. *Here I have discovered true wisdom that can only come from the Father of Lights. From each short story comes another gem of discovery, revealed by the Holy Spirit to one who is always searching for His guidance. In this short book I understand afresh how the God of the Universe desires to communicate to each one of us. Thank you, Barbara, for listening to the Spirit's nudging and sharing the revelations learned along the way."*

> Dr. Jim Strutz
> Teacher
> Founder of "Watch This!" local church
> Anchorage, Alaska

"What a fun, refreshing and encouraging book, full of great nuggets of wisdom and comfort. Barb tells her stories in a way we can all relate to, and she has a fun ribbon tying them all to Christ. While I was reading, I really felt the need to be more aware of my focus and what I am putting out to the atmosphere by what I choose to dwell on.

This book is bold. Barb shares her personal journey, and journal entries, to demonstrate how genuine and real a relationship with Christ is."

> Dia Matteson
> CEO and Owner of Harley-Davidson dealerships
> in Alaska and Arizona

"*Barbara's book* The Parable of the Fly *gives us hope for the future, with simple and clear truths to live by and keys to overcoming in these dark days! I love how Barbara gives us glimpses into her life during times of transition, that will help us have great grace in our own personal difficulties! These truths and authentic life stories will help us to shift forward as a unique son or daughter chosen by the King of kings.*"

> Eleanor Roehl
> Co-founder, Kingdom Warriors Alaska
> and Kingdom Alliance Network

"*I have been honored to read and comment on this book. Barbara is a seasoned woman of prayer who loves her Jesus, her husband Mike, her family, friends and Alaska with a passion and with Kingdom purpose. As you will soon read, her writings are full of rich wisdom, precious nuggets of truth, and deep insights into the very unusual circumstances of the last few years. Barbara weaves these illustrations together with her reflections from many decades of closeness with Jesus, and also adds insight into what is yet to come. I believe these writings will deepen your relationship with Jesus. There truly is a light of truth shining from each page.*

I can easily recommend this compilation of writings to both men and women, to people of all ages and in all stages of life, as I know that we have experienced many things in common during the events of the last few years. You will relate to and enjoy Barbara's writings. You will laugh and you may even cry, but for sure you will be inspired. You will also want to ponder the KEY take-aways at the end of every section. And if the title of the book is puzzling to you, please know that it's an important illustration to all that follows. I look forward to having this gem in my hands."

Mary Jill Callery
Missionary — Eastern Europe

ACKNOWLEDGMENTS

First of all, thank you Mike, my best friend and dear husband of 56 years. Wow, what a ride! You give your life to me and to our family in so many ways. You give loving framework and support for me to bravely spread my wings.

Thank you, Deborah Rubey and Brett Rawalt, for valuable help in editing this manuscript. Your extra sets of eyes on this writing have been priceless.

And thank you, Brett, for your extraordinary work in formatting, and doing the many aspects leading to the publishing of this book! Including the beautiful cover design and author photo. Such creative help in completing this project!

Thank you, my prayer-adventure friends — you keep JOY in the journey! There are too many of you to count — you know who you are. So valuable. Coffee meetups, sunset firepits, and Thai lunches — so many ways to bring fresh life!

Thank you, Father God — for weaving together these vignettes from such a wide span of years. It was so exciting to see the thread that connects them! Thank You, thank You – You write Your story in us, Your real LIFE.

INTRODUCTION

"How will it be when tough times come? How will we make it through?"

Important question.

This is the central question in the Prelude of this book, the original Parable from nearly 50 years ago.

That Parable asks this question; and the succeeding chapters, a collection of vignettes from a span of many years, give keys to answers. Those keys are even more vital now, when times have become tougher and this question has become even more pertinent.

So, how WILL we make it through?

Glimpses have come of timeless truths — valuable keys to strong and fruitful lives, to even thrive in the middle of trouble. Maybe *especially* in the middle of trouble!

The brief vignettes written here form an adventurous treasure hunt to true riches! At the end of each vignette, look for the keys!

May God give you true strength for the journey and joy in discovery!

Happy travels ~

PRELUDE
The Parable of the Fly

– APPROXIMATELY 1975 –

I was in the kitchen of our home in southern Arizona; doing dishes, and thinking through an interview I'd seen earlier that day on TV — an interview with Corrie ten Boom, a survivor of the Holocaust and well-respected author of *The Hiding Place*. She had spoken of great troubles the world would go through in coming years. And I was wondering, *"How will it be when times get rough? How will we make it through?"* And especially I was asking God, *"How will the young ones stand? How about the ones who will just have come to faith, to Christ, when those days come? How will THEY stand?"*

These were my thoughts in the kitchen that day. But just then, a fly came into the room, actually the biggest fly I'd ever seen! It was huge! It looked more like a fat bumble bee than a fly — and it buzzed loudly past my face on its way to the dining area, droning like a dive bomber! I grabbed a flyswatter to get this intruder, one so large that it felt like combat, like it was going to be it or me! Yet, I swiped ineptly at it and barely touched it.

But amazingly, it fell straight to the floor, dead! Dead-dead — Wow.

The thoughts that came quickly to me were very distinct:

> "That's who will fall — the 'fat and sassy ones,' boastful and proud, the ones who say, 'I'll never fall.' They will fall easily, and unexpectedly. But the young ones — they will know that they need help and will cry out to Me — and I will watch over them, so they will be fine. No, it's the other ones who will fall."

I've never forgotten the day that the God of the whole universe sent into my kitchen the biggest fly I'd ever seen — to answer a big question from this young Christian, a question very important to me. And I determined from that day on, to avoid being *"fat and sassy, boastful and proud"* — and instead my aim has been to be a "young one," wise enough to know that I need Him every hour.

* * *

** *I'm writing this postscript here nearly 50 years later, and I recall this lesson as one that's been foundational to my life. It rings true today, and instructs my way here in our current troubled times. The scene is dated, but the word I heard is timeless. It is so applicable to each of us in these days and onward.*

This Parable is the prelude to the following writings: words and pictures that show principles of life, and how to stand in all kinds of days, whether easy or extremely difficult. In these days and onward, we face both.

– *The Way Forward* –
Be a "young one" on an adventure.
Look for the keys!

1
One Thing

The first principle to know is: there is ONE THING.

It's highlighted here in my "life verse," Psalm 27:4:

> *"One thing have I asked of the Lord, that will I seek after: that I may dwell in the house of the Lord all the days of my life,*
> *to gaze upon the beauty of the Lord and to inquire in his temple."*

What is of primary importance?
Not several things — just one thing.
It's Him. God's own presence.
Really enjoying Him! … *It's the "beauty," not the "duty,"*
of the Lord.
Singular focus.

So many things try to grab our focus. And in the midst of trouble or crisis, that tendency is multiplied — so many voices cry loudly for our attention.

But any day, every day, through all the years, only one thing is central.

It's Him. Our Father God.

Young ones know that it's all about Daddy. They keep it simple.

KEY #1 – Keep singular focus and clear aim.

1975 THROUGH 1981

So many changes. From the sunny Arizona kitchen of "The Parable of the Fly," to other far-flung places where we moved as my husband's military career continued. Years that stretched our first-hand knowledge of US geography! But the truths from the Parable, to be teachable and lean into Father God, were applicable in each setting we encountered.

Washington DC area was the setting for the following writing, in the midst of further change. I was about to begin working very full days in a school in the busy city, and commuting on unaccustomed routes with a carload of children. Every part of this busy routine was a huge stretch for me.

The words I heard, which I call "Quiet Center," were distinct and practical. I applied them each day, as He carried me through such busy times.

They were survival words then, so long ago — and I share them here because they still are.

2
Quiet Center

– 1981 –

These were clear instructions I heard in my heart:

> *"Cultivate the quiet center of you. Come into the quiet, and share the quiet with Me.*
>
> *Cultivate, and greatly prize, this quiet center. It is more precious than rubies, more beautiful than diamonds. It is your stability in the midst of strife. It is your wellspring of joy, of peace, of hope — it is your life. Guard it carefully — do not let anyone or anything rob you of this precious resource.*
>
> *Welcome, and drink in, of My presence in you. Start the day with Me, and end the day with Me, and take Me as breaks in between.*
>
> *Meet with Me in the quiet — I love to meet with you. Let Me have your joys, your frustrations, your worries. Give*

them to Me. All else that is necessary will follow. All that is not necessary will fall away.

Let My peace garrison and mount guard over your heart as you trust in Me."

It was in the quiet times with Him that I heard Him even in busy days.

Humbly leaning into Him. Such a key to true strength.

KEY #2 – *Treasure what He treasures. Listen.*

1981 THROUGH 1989

From "survival in the DC city," to the warm sunshine of Southwest US, to the far north of Alaska — nothing moderate about those changes! It was true that our moves were all cross-country! The geography lesson continued, and we met so many people from such a rich variety of cultures and ways of life. The stretching was at so many levels.

Whether changes of location or climates or cultures, they can all be unsettling. Maybe that's the point. Un-settling. So many times of feeling shaken and uprooted, needing to trust Father God even more deeply.

A "survival journal" is where I collected scriptures pertinent to the needs of the times. That journal is where I kept many of the vignettes you are reading now in this book.

Then in the late 1980s, I would encounter a huge challenge. I wrote about it in the following story, "Towny Girl in the Woods."

3
Towny Girl in the Woods

– NEW YEAR'S DAY, 1990 –

Serious, dangerous cold. Don't-breathe-it-in, freeze-your-face cold. It's fifty-five degrees below zero, and nothing is moving. I grab my warmest scarf to cover my face; my breath frosts the scarf as I venture outside our newly-built log home. NOTHING moving. A dense ice fog shrouds the yard in ethereal mystery, as ice crystals hang suspended in the air. The look of an eerie movie scene. Our cars are frozen. And despite my husband Mike's most inventive efforts, those cars are going nowhere. No phone — no land lines, and it's before our days of cell phones. No lifeline. So, no way to call out and say, "Sorry, can't come. It's fifty-five below and my car is frozen."

No way out — and no way to tell anyone that. Within me, a knot tightens in the pit of my stomach. Tears are stinging and freezing on my cheeks. Isolated, and feeling helpless. Our family, and the wilderness. And my thought, *"So this is Mars."* Or, the Alaskan woods. A perfect storm — so many of my fears all rolled up together. So many unknowns, and I know so little. *"Can I actually live… here??! And how did I get here anyway…??"*

* * *

It was always his dream — for Mike, my dear husband of many years. It was his dream — but it wasn't my dream. Oh sure, Alaska was beautiful, and I did love living here. The landscape, so stunning, so big and wide and wild. I took hundreds of photos and stopped at every scenic viewpoint. And I loved the people we met: adventurous people, many quite different from ones I'd known in my growing up years in Fargo, North Dakota. I had also liked the places we lived along the way, in our 21+ military years — Indiana, Kansas, Washington state, Arizona, DC-area Virginia and New Mexico. Then we came to Fort Greely, way out in the Interior of Alaska — the really cold part. The "out-there-out-there" part. We'd been stationed at Fort Greely once before and knew we liked it. Yes, seriously, we did. But the dream — the dream persisted in Mike: that of building our own log home and living out in the woods. Not far from the small community of Delta Junction, and not too far off a small established road — but it felt really far out to me.

Yes, I had lived in those many states, had grown in many ways, and had enjoyed meeting people from lots of areas and cultures. Because bottom-line, I like people. And I had changed quite a bit from the quite-settled girl, from the quite-settled family in the flat and stable landscape of Fargo. And yet, even with all the changes through the years, I was still basically a "towny girl" — not really a country girl, let alone a wilderness girl. And I had never lived in the woods. On our own generator power. And in the beginning, with no phone line. Well, we did have a phone "connection point," but it was in the ditch a mile away, beside the established road: a bring-your-own-phone-and-plug-it-in place. Quite disconcerting to my mom and dad in Fargo, when I would call and say, "I only have a few minutes to talk, because I'm in the ditch — and it's cold out here!"

The dream. I wanted Mike to be able to actually DO this dream that he'd envisioned for years. And so, we began: we and our two teenaged sons downed trees, using a chain saw and the winch on our truck, preparing for the homesite driveway. What a big, brave project! Through the long clearing and building time, I did a few basic house building tasks, but mostly I brought sandwiches and milkshakes to the workers and helpers who were often family and friends, the many who assisted in this huge project. It took three summers of work to bring the log home to completion. Sitting in the midst of large stands of birch and spruce, the log home was beautiful. It looked like a lodge, a retreat setting.

But as the time approached to move from our comfortable military quarters at Fort Greely to this new home in the woods, I fought fears — capital letter FEARS. Many kinds of fears: of the remoteness, and of unaccustomed power systems — a big generator we named Bertha (who had her own shed) and what's an inverter??!! Fear of having no phone line at the house, making us unreachable for my parents in Fargo, for our older son at college in Seattle, and for our younger son, who daily drove to the town high school on our fledgling self-maintained road. And of course, fear of bears. They were in our neighborhood — oh let's face it, we were in THEIR neighborhood!! And there was the persistent question deep inside: *"What if I can't actually DO this Dream?* Oh God, HELP!"

We moved in before Christmas and began the learning curve of life in the woods. As I mentioned here, News Year's Day was a big test. The temperature, fifty-five below zero — and us without a garage for our seriously-freezing cars. Inventive methods were employed in an attempt to thaw them out enough to start; but that day, nothing worked. I faced a very cold reality: going nowhere, with no way to let anyone know that. Just one of the many moments of feeling quite helpless.

After a few weeks, though, we did get a phone line back to our house. In a group project, Mike and a few friends dragged a phone line by snowmachine over the one mile of deep snow and wooded terrain. After a few initial glitches, it worked. A miracle! So many daunting things, beginning our many years in that house in the woods.

As I adapted to life there, I did see some wonderful things: great clarity of the night sky, and watching (and even hearing) the aurora dance across it. Most notable to me was the amazing quiet — I joked that I could hear if a bird switched branches. Over time, something inside of me quieted too along with the landscape. And the love of that quiet increased in me.

Part of our life in the woods: we started a garden — a project that was definitely larger than our expertise! It looked formidable, with a tall moose fence around it to guard the precious rows and rows of more veggies than we could ever eat! Mercifully, it grew and even prospered, impressive for these beginner gardeners! Our favorites were broccoli and snow peas, and the many rows of raspberry canes that took over more area with each passing season. Another favorite part of life there was riding our 4-wheelers around the 320-acre property. And although at first our closest neighbor was about a mile away, we later had neighbors as close as a third of a mile, practically next door!

And we were not hermits — we hosted many guests and occasional group gatherings at our house. Some people came for what we called "hunt camp" during the fall moose season. Some came from city places far away; one young man from Chicago, Steve, stayed with us one fall for several days. We noticed that he got up early in the morning and just walked quietly all around our large yard. He later remarked that he hoped we realized how unique and special this place was.

Many years later, we moved to the "big city" of Anchorage to be closer to our sons — and by then, also daughter-in-law and grandkids. And while I liked being back in the city, I often missed the quiet. But one day as I was praying about that, I saw a scene in my heart — it was summer, a warm sunny day, and I was sitting on the shaded front porch of the house in the woods. It was quiet, so very quiet — and I could hear the birds switching branches and chirping cheerfully. A happy scene. Then I heard a short song with a lilting tune, *"Sittin' sippin' lemonade with You, on the front porch, on the front porch."* And God whispered to my heart,

> "The quiet. You can go there anytime. I built it in you, I weaved it inside you, in that time. Yes, THAT time. That time in the woods. That time you were afraid of. The quiet, and this scene — it's in you now."

Such a scene — my reminder of that time in the woods. Reminder of great treasure.

No, it wasn't my dream — but it became my treasure.

* * *

Now many years later, I look back at that time of being that "towny girl" in the woods. What I shared here from our beginnings showed the "perfect storm." So many fears all rolled up together. Some of mine were: fear of wilderness; of bears and other animals; of separation from kids and other family; of mechanical things — crucial ones that were a mystery to me; fear of other unknowns; fear of cold, and crazy-cold; and the biggest for me, fear of isolation and THE unknown itself. My time there gave me huge opportunities for overcoming. Somehow, in facing those fears and leaning into Jesus for His strength, I grew on the inside. His strength became mine. Later, when I moved on, I was stronger than if I hadn't faced the fears.

My years in the woods together with my loving guy Mike, remind me of Psalm 84:5-7:

> "Blessed are those whose strength is in you, in whose hearts are the highways to Zion. As they go through the Valley of Baca [weeping] they make it a place of springs; the early rain also covers it with pools. They go from strength to strength; each one appears before God in Zion."

Later in our years of living there, that very place where I faced so many fears became a source place, a house of blessing to multiplied others. Many people who came there found warmth and respite and a place of peace. To a young woman, Rachel, who needed a home for a month or so, it was a place of personal breakthrough and restoration. To a family, Serge and Nadia and their four littles, who were new there from another culture, it was a safe and warm home while they worked on theirs.

And to us they brought new language & food experiences, and we became like extended family! To my sister Marlene, who came from out of state for many visits, it was a place of refreshing and peace. To the many who came from a variety of local church groups to our periodic "picnic and praise" gatherings, it was a place of joy in Christian community. There were so many ways of blessing, in that place. Wow — the place of facing fears became the place of both giving and receiving blessing.

But I wonder, how about you? What are your fears? They may be different than mine. Some fears are common, like fears of isolation and bears and other dangers; other fears can be more unique. It's valuable to think them through, not only surface fears but ones that are underneath. Facing those fears in Jesus can bring new strength on the inside, and lead forward into increasingly productive, joyful life!

*KEY #3 – Face the fears.
Look for the gifts.*

4
Change and the City

– 2005 –

After all the years of life in the woods of Interior Alaska, our move to "the big city" of Anchorage was another big switch. "Towny Girl" was back in town! What could be hard about that? And yet, after 15 years in the woods, it was still another brave time.

Yes, I had desired and really welcomed being near our sons and daughter-in-law and grandkids. The location not far from both mountains and ocean was a beautiful blend. And the slightly milder climate was definitely a plus. All this was inviting.

But… change. It was still something to deal with.

The biggest difference I noticed was the greatly diminished personal space. From the large log home in the woods, with spacious lot and 30 acres of our own, the nearest neighbor being a third of a mile away; to now a crowded cul-de-sac, with neighbors so close all around us and nearly deck-to-deck in the back. Friendly neighbors, to be sure… but close!

Another big difference was complexity. The marketplace, with so many choices! From formerly going shopping in the nearby small town, getting groceries at THE grocery store, with any further choices 100 miles up the road! To now here in the city, with several choices for groceries within a few blocks of our home. Or want hardware? From the small town's two choices, to here with multiple choices. That change to multiple options seemed subtle at first, but it added layers of complexity to everyday decisions — and a big adjustment for daily life.

Also, here in my downsized, light, bright, distinctly non-log home, my "little house on the cul-de-sac," the quiet. Oh yes, the quiet — that was hard to find. From formerly hearing birds switch branches, to now hearing voices echo across the neighborhood. My appreciation for quiet, which had developed significantly in my years in the woods — the quiet was what I missed the most.

Years later, we would move to a more wooded area in the Anchorage hillside, but for these first eight years in the city, lack of quiet was my world.

There were certainly pluses — being with family members in normal settings, and not only on special occasions with their compressed visit times. That was essentially why we had moved here.

I was reminded of that value, "the why" of our move to the city: for intentional time to affect and bless our generations. HUGE value! And it's been so worth it. I was reminded too that God would show the ways to adapt in this new day of a different environment. He had shown me how to do this in the many moves in the past, and He would show me again.

I reached for the adjustment tools He showed me. One tool was a more defined quiet time. I realized that even in the country, I hadn't needed ALL time to be quiet, just some time. New habits developed: of deliberate, focused time, a dial-down time at night; and frequent daytime prayer drives, especially down the nearby Inlet to take in the scene. I also saw with freshness the beauty here, the majestic mountains and nearby Inlet views. And I recognized rich community in this new settling, the new church family that we loved. Those choices helped me anchor here more quickly.

So, the challenges I faced: the complexity — I found simplicity could not depend on the world around me, but that there were ways to keep that simple time in my heart. And the lack of personal space — I learned to keep more intentional boundaries, and to define my own space.

Reminders: In days of change, I looked for the anchor, and anchored into Him. I asked for His help, and looked to His Word, and listened. One scripture particularly helped me — Isaiah 42:10:

> "Sing to the Lord a new song, his praise from the end of the earth, you who go down to the sea, and all that fills it, the coastlands and their inhabitants."

Here I was, in new days, down at the sea, down to the coastlands, and realizing He would give me that new song!

I asked also for His lens, for me to see the new possibilities. And for keys, even little things that would help to navigate the new waters.

The things I learned then, in 2005 in the big switch from country to city, helped in the myriad of changes that would come in succeeding years. They can help even now — to help me, and you too, in any changes and even big shifts we're encountering.

KEY #4 – Look for the tools God gives.

5
Do You Know...
Who You Are?

– APPROXIMATELY 2017 –

That big change of moving from the woods of Interior Alaska to the "big city" of Anchorage also marked the beginning of some different styles of vacation, with annual vacation trips to a new favorite resort in Mazatlán, Mexico. That is the scene, several years later, of this writing:

We were approaching the landing zone near Mazatlán airport — what a welcome sight, as I looked over the landscape and fields outside the city. Mike and I had been here several times before, to this favorite springtime vacation place. I was just resting for a moment, anticipating the busyness of the airport, and customs; then the taxi ride, and sights and sounds of the busy streets of Mazatlán.

We were in our final descent when I heard a clear word to my heart: *"Do you know… that when you land here, the atmosphere of Mazatlán changes?"*

"What??" I thought about that, and answered, *"Well, I guess so... I mean, You live in me and You're the King, and where You go, Your presence changes the place... So, I guess so."*

But the phrase continued in my thoughts: *"Do. you. know... the atmosphere changes."* Hmm...

The next day, we talked about it again. And I thought it through some more.

"Do you know... who you are... because of Whose you are?" Again, I answered: *"In my head, yes, I 'know' it. But since You asked the question, I guess I don't know it like You'd want me to know it. Help me Lord, to KNOW it!"*

A question — I love that He brings a question. A question invites dialogue and interaction. It reminds me that I'm a daughter of a Father who invites me into relationship that has dimension to it! It's not just static statements and "right answers."

So, do I know, not only the right answer, but deep down do I KNOW this, in the sense of *"I can walk this out!"* KNOWING is like a deep awareness that affects not only my thinking but my heart.

I also heard, *"You have authority here — you have land, and much people in this place."* Land? Well, I do have a "piece of property," a timeshare! And yes, we do know many who live here, who we interact with whenever we come. But wow, authority in this place. I continued thinking on that as well.

I was reminded of some scriptures:

In Joshua 1:3, Joshua was told by God that he had authority where he walked:

> *"Every place that the sole of your foot will tread upon I have given to you, just as I promised to Moses..."* And in verse 9: *"...be strong and courageous. Do not be frightened, and do not be dismayed, for the Lord your God is with you wherever you go."*

2 Corinthians 2:14-15:

> *"...thanks be to God, who in Christ always leads us in triumphal procession, and through us spreads the fragrance of the knowledge of him everywhere..."* (His Presence in us spreads through us, wherever we go.)

And in the book of Acts, a mob of Jews were speaking to the authorities at Thessalonica, here in Acts 17:6:

> *"These men who have turned the world upside down have come here also..."* (A reminder that not all will be pleased with those atmosphere changes!)

Romans 8:15 talks about our relationship with God in adoption as true sons and daughters of our Father. Not only with God the King, but with God our Father who wants relationship. The One who asks me a question, because He wants to hear my thoughts. I can engage with Him!

"Do. You. Know?" (You change the atmosphere, where you go.) That springtime in Mazatlán, that question affected me a lot. I felt different, with somehow a sense of greater perspective, through my two weeks there. I walked more confidently, not

arrogantly, but more than a tourist; rather, as a person with ownership. I walked with mindfulness and more sense of purpose in my interactions there.

But it's not only me, and not only Mazatlán. This question can engage each of us wherever we go. If we know that because of Him we affect the world around us, and His presence in us shifts the atmosphere, what a difference that can make in our days!

How does knowing this affect our days? Our outlook?

Realizing (and here making it personal):

1. I set the atmosphere of my home, whether I'm alone or with others living there.
2. I set the atmosphere at my workplace or other daily arena.
3. In the marketplace, I affect that interaction with the store clerk, and with others who I meet.

Realizing that His presence in me affects the world I encounter; He leads me to steward this privilege in a more mindful way. How about you?

KEY #5 – *Realize God-in-us makes a whole world of difference.*

6
A Question

- 2017 -

I love that God opened the conversation with a question. Like that time that I just referred to, as we were landing in Mazatlán, when He asked, *"Do you know… that when you land, the atmosphere changes?"*

"Do you know…?"

I really LOVE that it's a question! A question — an invitation to dialogue, in a relationship that is dynamic. Dialogue, and interaction. Not a static statement, not a stand-alone pronouncement.

In fact, in the Prelude of this book, the opening piece of *The Parable of the Fly,* there was my question: *"How will it be when times get rough??"* And then His answer, which was both immediate and long-term, that He is still answering! What an adventure!

Jesus, You invite us into relationship, interactively meeting together! Thank You that it's ok to ask questions, and even to wrestle with things — this relationship is alive!

God asking me a question reminds me that I'm not only a daughter of the King. I'm a daughter of a Father who invites me into a relationship that is dynamic! Way beyond just flat statements and "right answers," this relationship has depth and dimension!

Walking with You in a living interaction that's full of life — what a strength.

KEY #6 – *Keep interacting with Him, in relationship that is alive!*

2018 AND ONWARD

2018, a pivotal point — for me personally, times of more upheaval began. A combination of a personal health crisis (severe shingles on head and face with ongoing nerve pain) and soon after, a very unsettling crisis at our local church. So much shaking of stability and relationships. Shaking, and then unraveling. Many steadying scriptures and words became even more valuable than before.

I don't know about your days and years, but it does seem there are "hotter" times, more trying times, that come to us all. Many types of crises and challenges, times when being well anchored is even more crucial. Times when normal "daily bread" days become "savor the last morsel" days.

2018 and onward were like that for me. And because God is so faithful, He brought even clearer word than in any other time. Many of those vital words are in the following vignettes, bringing precious messages that gave courage.

Faithful Father God — He will bring words to you too: just ask Him. And then, lean in and listen.

He brings fresh bread.

7
There is a River

― SPRING OF 2018 ―

In contrast to the beautiful springtime, there was great shaking in our personal, local church world. This scripture came strongly to mind at that time, and it was such a steadying word. I wrote these insights then:

Psalm 46 — what a strength this scripture brings, especially in these days of shaking and upheaval. Look at this goldmine! It's brought great strength to me, and perhaps it will to you too. Here it is. Psalm 46:1-3:

> "God is our refuge and strength, a very present help in trouble. Therefore, we will not fear, though the earth gives way, though the mountains be moved into the heart of the sea, though its waters roar and foam, though the mountains tremble at its swelling. Selah."

Such a reminder to know the true source: our source of refuge, strength, and help. Then we can know stability.

Even in cataclysmic change, unsettling in the extreme — earth-shaking, foundation-shaking, when the potential for fear is HIGH.

> Verse 4: *"There is a river whose streams make glad the city of God, the holy habitation of the Highest."*

"There is a river…" This statement is such a direct contrast, a whole different tone to the tumult of the previous verses. Here is a whole separate ecosystem! What a GREAT discovery! The true source of strength, and even the source of health and joy — it's HIM! He's the River. We can not only survive in this separate environment; we can actually *thrive!*

> Verse 5: *"God is in the midst of her; she shall not be moved; God will help her when morning dawns."*

Because He is in our midst, this set-apart place will not be shaken. God will help His own home!

> Verse 6: *"The nations rage, the kingdoms totter; He utters His voice, the earth melts."*

Even more shaking, more widespread, going on.
It was bad, and then… it got worse!

> Verse 7: *"The Lord of hosts is with us; the God of Jacob is our fortress. Selah."*

Even with all that widespread shaking, the truth is, the Lord of hosts, the Commander of heaven's armies, is WITH us — He Himself is our fortress, our "safe house."

> Verse 8: *"Come, behold the works of the Lord, how he has brought desolations on the earth. He makes wars cease to the end of the earth; He breaks the bow and shatters the spear; He burns the chariots with fire."*

He invites us to come and see what He sees and what He does. When He says war is done, it's DONE!! He breaks the weaponry, burns the chariots, the enemy equipment, their shields and mobility, because HE is in charge!

> Verse 9: *"Be still, and know that I am God. I will be exalted among the nations; I will be exalted in the earth!"*

It's important to pause and realize, He alone is God — He rules, and He wins! And when we realize this, we can stop our fearful striving.

> Verse 10, *"The Lord of hosts is with us; the God of Jacob is our fortress."*

Lest we forget, the Commander over all commanders is with us. Bottom Line: He is our fortress. His own presence is our safe house, our real home.

This Psalm was GOLD to me, and it's why I wrote it out in detail. Because it was, and still is, such an anchoring truth, in the midst of all kinds of shaking. Whether that upheaval is personal, local, or global — He is the One who is in charge.

He is the Only One not shaking.

***KEY #7** – Live at the River, His separate ecosystem.*

8
Mudflats

– SUMMER OF 2018 –

In the midst of continuing upheaval, I wrote of this scene:

I saw a very important scene the other day. This summer has been a notable time, so challenging. One day in July, I was driving north from Seward to Anchorage and came along Cook Inlet.

I saw an unusual scene: miles and miles of mudflats, indicating a very extreme minus tide. And further on, I was there at the right moment to see a bore tide: like a formidable wave of incoming water — a thrilling sight!

I'd seen a bore tide once before. That former time had included a word to my heart, about a large "tide" of people who would be coming into the kingdom of God. So, when I saw this recent tide, I was reminded of that previous *"people are coming"* word.

But this time there was an additional thought: *right before an extreme tide, a bore tide, is an extreme minus tide* — the miles and miles of mudflats I had just seen. With that thought of mudflats was the sense of *"you are there."* An encouragement of sorts, to realize that in the tough days we were in, to not give up during this "mudflats time." A tide would be coming; a big one.

Principles came to mind, that here I'm calling *"Things to Know About Mudflats:"*

1. *Mudflats are not pretty.* They are barren, exposed, mucky. No photographers are lining up for the mudflat photos.

2. *Mudflats are dangerous!* People in coastal areas have seen the signs, and know (or should know) they are warnings to not walk just anywhere around mudflats. Caution and carefulness are crucial anywhere around them. Because mudflats kill — they swallow people! So, carefulness is needed to avoid getting feet caught in the muck. So, the warning I felt in me was that *especially in a mudflats time, don't get into the muck.* Or figuratively, it's not a time to pick up mud, or offenses, from myself or others. That's way too expensive — my heart surely could not afford it.

3. *Mudflats precede another tide.* So, if I were a fisherman, I'd be using this time, this barren and mucky-sucky time, to get my nets ready! I would not be swayed by what the surroundings look like, but would realize that with a minus tide this big, the tide that's coming will also be big, with lots of fish. I would be prepping my nets, and tightening the knots. The knots, a picture of both vertical God-connection, and horizontal connection with others. And I'd be clearing up any snarls or

disconnects in my nets, checking for any holes in them. Really a heart-check time — all to have my nets ready, and to be prepared for the big tide.

4. *Reminder:* the same God who brought me past the mudflats, and then had me at the right place at the right time for the thrilling moment of the bore tide, has got each of us. *He is the King of Tides.* He's got this, and we can trust Him.

Seeing this perspective in mucky times can help give both caution and hope, when we need it most.

KEY #8 – *In mucky days, watch our steps!*

9
Steady in Unsteady Times: Oh Jude!

– SUMMER OF 2018 –

The book of Jude. A book written in times of trouble, addressed to a "trouble" bunch. Surely there are things to glean here!

Even though sent to a "trouble bunch," the book of Jude is addressed to the *"called, beloved… and kept."*

Most of the book speaks of days of darkness, deception, discord, and division — hmm, sounds a lot like our world today!

But finally, there's a switch of tone, a contrast to all the previous verses, here in verse 20: *"But you, BELOVED…"* Remember? Verse 1 called them that! Oh yes, that's who we really are too — BELOVED.

One key to steadiness: knowing who we really are. "Beloved" is our true name.

Who we know we are — that's how we can walk. Not trying to BE someone, but walking in who we really know we are.

The term *Beloved* continues in verse 20:

> *"But you, Beloved, building yourselves up in your most holy* [set apart] *faith…"* (being strengthened on the inside) *"…praying in the Holy Spirit…"* (as led by the Holy Spirit.)

In other words, *"Father, I give You my heart! What is Your prayer? Please pray Your prayer through me!"* (Whether in our native language or in spiritual, prayer language.)

Verse 21: *"Keep yourselves in the love of God…"* We were already called *"kept,"* but here is also mentioning a choice — to keep ourselves in the love of God. In the circle of His love, to live outward from there, from a base of love instead of fear.

One expression of fear is self-protection — so, healing from fear can also bring freedom in our hearts!

As we are strengthened on the inside, praying under His direction, and making choices that keep us in the love circle rather than the fear circle — regular life choices continue. But if we're in that strengthened place, then we can reach out to others from healthy motives. Standing in love, and released from fear and self-protection, we are free to reach out to others in wisdom and for their benefit, rather than for our need to "look good."

The ending of Jude is a great big promise, in verses 24-25: *"Now to Him who is able to keep you from stumbling ... to Him be glory..."* What beautiful assurance!

There are so many keys in this little book of Jude. God brings warnings about things to watch out for; and also brings direction on how we can be strengthened. Instructions on how to stay in His circle of love and be free from fear — that's so crucial!

I wrote some thoughts about Jude 21, called *"Choices:"*

> *Self builds walls where none are needed;*
> *Leaves giant gaps where walls are crucial;*
> *And does not well discern the difference.*
> *God knows well what and how to protect,*
> *And I can trust Him.*

KEY #9 – *Counter the culture.*
Pray.
Strengthen on the inside.

10
Wear These Truths

– JANUARY 2019 –

New year — continuation of a shaking time personally, but also a full year before a worldwide shaking, the well-known global pandemic time. I saw this mental image, and heard a word that accompanied it.

The view was of a necklace. It was very beautiful — a simple, jewel-neck style, a single strand of sparkling gems, alternating deep royal blue and sparkling clear crystal. They were notably dazzling, sparkling gems. This picture came with a distinct phrase, *"You. Will. Need. This."* Slow and emphasized like that. What could it mean? It sounded important! So, I thought it through. The deep blue color reminded me of royalty, and of who we are in Him; and the sparkling clear crystal spoke to me of His purity, and of clarity and honest reality.

Proverbs 3:3 says,

> "Let not steadfast love and faithfulness forsake you; bind them around your neck; write them on the tablet of your heart."

What I saw was this: to wear God's own character like a necklace, so that it would remind us of His anchoring, His steady love and faithfulness.

And to write those truths on our hearts, as in, *"Don't lose them, commit them to memory."* A reminder that they are so vital, they should never be lost or misplaced. They should be an anchor.

I had actually seen this same picture and phrase three different times in 2018. The first time was early in the year, before the shake-up at our local church. The second time was one day before Anchorage experienced a significant 7.1 earthquake, on November 30. And the third time was this time, as we entered 2019.

So, into that year, and succeeding years, went this anchoring truth. A visual reminder to hang on to this: His steady love, and His faithfulness. Far more real than anything we would encounter. And as it turns out, we still need this word.

Wear these truths. Let His own character be our anchor.

KEY #10 – Wear this: His steady love and faithfulness.

11
Year of the Dance
Part 1

– SPRING OF 2019 –

The figurine was of a lovely dancing girl. She was bought in Mazatlán, a birthday gift from my dear sister as we browsed in a favorite shop that springtime day. I carefully carried that figurine on the plane ride, all the way home to Alaska. Then, as I placed her on a featured shelf near my prayer corner, a clear phrase came to mind: *"This is the Year of the Dance!"*

As days went on and I continued to pray in that corner, the phrase and the graceful figurine impressed me even more. Because it had been a time, a long time it seemed, that I'd been realizing a need in me for healing — healing of my heart. It had been over a year of notable pain and loss, in our local community, with much pain in my own heart.

Part 1 — Receiving —
The familiar story of the Good Samaritan was related at our church. (Luke 10:25-37) There are at least six main characters in the story. At least two robbers; one man who's been robbed and left for dead; one priest; one Levite (Jewish religious per-

son) and one Samaritan. (In the culture of the day, a Samaritan was seen by "true Jews" as a half-breed, and was hated.)

Often when this famous story is shared, we're left trying to decide if we are the priest (religious leader, who ignores the man in need) the Levite (religious worker, who does the same) or the Samaritan (in this story, the "good guy," the one who cares and reaches out to help.) We usually think of only those three characters.

But as I prayed in my corner, I suddenly saw another view of this. A surprising view of an often-forgotten person in this story: I saw that I was "the person in the ditch." That the enemy of my soul had robbed me of life and hope — that's always the enemy's gameplan. And just as in this story, I was helpless to bring myself to healing. But I saw that Jesus came down, and He took on the role of the half-breed, the despised. Not the priest, and not the religious professional, but this One who took on being despised and hated. I saw Him come to where I was. He saw me and my deep needs, and had compassion — He really cared.

He not only cared in theory, but He bound up my wounds. Then He lavishly poured on the oil (His own presence and power) and wine (antiseptic and cleansing) and put me on His own donkey while He walked. He brought me to the Inn of His Presence, a place to stay long enough to heal thoroughly — as healing is a process, often needing extra time for thorough wholeness. And He paid the whole tab, the entire cost for my healing to be complete.

Wow, what a Savior!

The Year of the Dance, Part 1 — begins here, at the Inn of His Presence, receiving from Him.

KEY 11 – *Wounds happen. Take time for healing in His presence.*

12
Year of the Dance
Part 2

In Part 1, the Year of the Dance began with receiving. It began in me, with my admission that I was in need and willing to receive His caring touch: first at the scene of robbery and injury, and later at the Inn of His Presence, receiving healing from Him.

Hmm... *receiving*. That time of receiving does not come easily for me, or for many of us. We are much more comfortable with giving and doing and feeling accomplished; and measuring ourselves often to see how we're doing in that business of doing!

But receiving? Not so much. Not so comfortable, especially if it takes a while. That may seem like a waste of time.

But I invite you, friend, to join me here in this Year of the Dance, as this process can be a present-tense reality!

Part 2 — First Steps —

Here in Year of the Dance, Part 2, that uncomfortable thought of receiving continues. Coming from the Inn of His Presence, the place of receiving healing and strength, into this new part, taking the first steps of dance — but with a little different picture than expected.

The emphasis is on moving in step with Him from a place of rest. Yes, from a place of REST, rather than from a place of stressful, task-oriented, obligatory "doing." Once again there's the reminder, as so many of us are more comfortable with *doing* than *being*.

But here in my prayer corner, I'm reminded, as I glance at my dancing girl figurine — I see the gracefulness of her dance, seamlessly in step with the song. Such an ease and flow to that dance. I'm reminded of the scripture — some familiar words about resting in Him and following His lead.

Here it is, in The Message Version (MSG), Jesus speaking in Matthew 11:28-30:

> *"Are you tired? Worn out? Burned out on religion? Come to me. Get away with me and you'll recover your life. I'll show you how to take a real rest. Walk with me and work with me — watch how I do it. Learn the unforced rhythms of grace. I won't lay anything heavy or ill-fitting on you. Keep company with me and you'll learn how to live freely and lightly."*

Hmm... *"Learn the unforced rhythms of grace."* Learn. Sounds like it doesn't come naturally, since it must be learned; and Jesus is saying that He's the teacher.

But it does sound like a dance, doesn't it? The effortless kind, like the dancing girl.

So, in this Year of the Dance, Part 2, is His invitation, learning from Him *"the unforced rhythms of grace."*

Beautiful when we get used to it.
He sees the beauty already.

KEY #12 – Practice
"...the unforced rhythms of grace."

13
Year of the Dance
Part 3

Looking back, Part 1 of this theme was about acknowledging my need and receiving healing from God at the Inn of His Presence. (From Luke 10:25-37)

And Part 2 was about taking steps, beginning to dance in step with Him from a place of rest rather than obligation. (From Matthew 11:28-30)

The Year of the Dance — Part 3
This final part is about moving into fresh joy, the dance of freedom. An enthusiastic great big *celebration* with this dance!!

I'm sharing these thoughts because although this process has been personal, I believe that the principles I saw are applicable in general. So many of us are in unusual and challenging times; and what I saw is a valuable process of healing and freedom.

I'm reminded that each of us are unique in how we walk through times of mourning and grieving, facing places of loss.

Walking through that takes time. I too have been learning that it is good and healthy to acknowledge that grieving, and to walk through it to full healing.

Here's a dynamite verse about that! Psalm 30:11 (NLT):

> *"You have turned my mourning into joyful dancing. You have taken away my clothes of mourning and clothed me with joy."*

Can you imagine?! He takes the raw material of my mourning and turns it into joyful dancing!! Not your average exchange!! Wow!!

I look again at my dancing girl figurine, the beautiful birthday gift, and I notice the color of her dress. It's a stunning burnished red. It looks like a fitting JOY color, possibly a red that's come through fire! What a picture of release and freedom! And her step is a bit tilted — she's leaning forward just enough to necessitate change, to initiate the next step.

And her hands are lifted up, touching her broad-brimmed hat; like she's gracefully moving in alignment with her covering, her Lord. A picture of joyful surrender.

A scripture speaks about this, Ecclesiastes 3:1,4:

> *"For everything there is a season, and a time for every matter under heaven… there's a time to weep, and a time to laugh… a time to mourn, and a time to dance."*

The dancing girl, this lovely figurine, gives that beautiful picture.

It seems she is announcing a new season! And she is moving in agreement with her lead, her Lord — moving in dance and joy and release!

Thank You, Father, for the healing journey you had planned as I walked the streets of Mazatlán that day and saw this beautiful figurine, the dancing girl. I didn't know all that You would bring from her graceful dance.

Like the joyful expression in this figurine, I now say to myself, and to you too, *"Happy Year of the Dance!!"*

Joy and freedom! — He's the One to bring this, a thorough process.

KEY #13 – *Dance freely and celebrate His grace!*

14
Onramps

– JUNE 2019 –

Still in the middle of unsettled days here in our local connection circles. So many changes. One day, I was driving on a local highway when I noticed a new exit. Curious about where it led, I got off there and drove around the newly constructed traffic circle. How fun! Right about then, I heard this word to my heart:

> *"I am building brand-new onramps, to meet with you in brand-new ways. And I am shaking up your status quo, so that you will know — I am not contained by what you call 'familiar.'"*

Hmm…. what?? Onramps sounded exciting, though mysterious. But shaking up my status quo… not sure. So, I looked up "status quo," and it's defined as *"the existing state of affairs, the present situation."* In other words, *"the way things are."* Sounded like a comfort zone to me! And the onramps? I pictured a construction zone, and orange cones! At least it spoke of this change as having a purpose, probably good. And the purpose, to meet with Him in new ways. The goal, to know Him better — ok, that's always worth it.

But *"the way things are"* — things I get used to, even things I like. It could involve all of that. And more stretch. I knew I had gone through many changes, and yet was still quite a stability-loving person.

Not long after that June day, a scripture stood out to me — one I laughingly called the "No One Puts This on Their Fridge Scripture!" Here it is, Isaiah 42:13-16:

> *"The Lord goes out like a mighty man, like a man of war he stirs up his zeal;*
> *He cries out, he shouts aloud; he shows himself mighty against his foes.*
> *For a long time I have held my peace; I have kept still and restrained myself; now I will cry out like a woman in labor; I will gasp and pant.*
>
> *I will lay waste mountains and hills, and dry up all their vegetation; I will turn the rivers into islands, and dry up the pools."* (like 'change the whole landscape' — sounds like a construction zone!)
>
> *"…And I will lead the blind in a way that they do not know, in paths that they have not known I will guide them. I will turn the darkness before them into light, the rough places into level ground. These are the things I do, and I do not forsake them."*

Interesting passage! Surely not the serene *"He leads me beside the still waters"* section. No, this Isaiah 42 passage sounds loud and passionate, very intense. I pictured a whole construction zone; even mountains being leveled, a whole landscape being rearranged. And then there was the part about Him leading us into unfamiliar territory. But finally, some assurance: it's God doing the guiding, and turning darkness and obscurity into light.

I pictured that construction zone at night, with the pilot car, its lights on, leading vehicles through the rough terrain. And the rough areas were being turned into level ground. Then it ended with the best phrase, very comforting in the middle of all that change: *"…and I do not forsake them."* So glad for that, after some very intense movement going on!

But in looking at that scripture that speaks about huge change, a personal heart check is fitting:

1. *"Am I anchored to the landscape?"* — Because guess what, it's moving!

2. *"Am I anchored to the 'familiar'?"* (Also called "the way things are") — Because this scene does not look familiar!

3. *"Am I anchored, actually well-anchored, to Father God?"* — Important question, worth the recheck, because *He's the ONLY one steady* in this changing landscape.

The next verse, Isaiah 42:17, has an odd reference, a warning about idols. So, I asked the Lord a question about something I had never understood: *"Father, what is it with idols? What's the appeal of an idol?"*

An interesting answer came quickly:

> "It doesn't DO anything! You can stick it on a shelf and it doesn't move! It's very manageable. Predictable. That's its attraction. You can worship it and walk away, and it won't move!"

Wow! That's really different from the Living God, who invites me to live in active relationship with Him!

My prayer, in view of this God who speaks of change, even earth-moving change, was this: *"Father, I give you my heart, and any ties that have been anchored to my own landscape and my familiar scene. And I receive You, the Living God — Father, I anchor into You."*

* * *

In the following months, this passage made even more sense. There were our own personal changes, as we made a move to another local church in late fall and began to settle in a different spiritual environment. Then in the spring of 2020, we and the whole world encountered a great big change, the pandemic that brought such rapid widespread change. Ways of meeting changed, as zoom often replaced in-person meetings, and as we gathered in other outside-the-box places.

Wow, what a change of landscape! I remembered this scripture and this scene. And the reference to change and "the ways things are." This reminder was a comfort, and it really helped during all those transitions.

We don't know the many changes yet to come — but we do know He is the safe place to anchor in the midst of even earth-moving change. I wrote more on this topic as these pages continue. So much insight came in the midst of the great pressures we all felt, as we moved onward from the end of 2019.

But first, God reminded me of His faithfulness, His trustworthiness.

KEY #14 – Prep for change. Trust Him in "Wow, what a ride!"

15
Faithful God

– DECEMBER 2019 –

A big reminder came to me in the last month of the year. After a number of hard months (a large number!) I felt this nudge to my heart, and the term *"24 months."*

The words continued, *"It's been 24 months of word and picture and direction."* I felt reminded to look back in my own prayer journal. I looked and marveled at the amazing things that had happened, all in the midst of hardship. The rest of my reminder was to not only look for those words, but to stop and thank Him for them, and to collect them like I would gather stones for a memorial or altar.

So, I went on the treasure hunt! What I found was that all the way through the 24 months were quite distinct nudges and words that gave direction — notably more than in any previous timeframe. There were things I highlighted from each month, pivotal things. I won't belabor them, but one was a specific invitation early in 2018: *"Come up here and soar with*

Me… pray from My perspective," not long before our own local church world imploded.

And that word in summer of 2018. as I viewed those extensive mudflats I wrote about, essentially saying to *"watch your step, don't get sucked into the muck; use your time, prep for a big tide coming."* There was a word I shared with a group in late 2018, about *"being steady in unsteady times,"* just a few days before the 7.1 earthquake shook our world here in Anchorage, to be followed by several months of nerve-rattling aftershocks. Huge timeliness to those words!

A few months later, there was an amazingly reassuring picture and word about our identity as His beloved, part of a scene at a California vineyard. And in the fall of 2019, what I just wrote, about the onramps, and huge, messy change coming. But also, the assurance that in the middle of it, there would be new ways to meet with Him; there would be an upside to all that change. And now there was this, in December of 2019, the specific reminder to review what He had said, and to be keenly aware of His great faithfulness. To specifically thank Him. And even to note that thanks in some way — a special rock, or pile of rocks: something visual that would serve as a reminder.

All to remember — it had been 24 months of picture and word and direction.

All to celebrate His faithfulness!

That emphasis was distinct, as we entered the brave new world of 2020 — with much indication to prepare for new things. To accept the invitation into days of adventure, seeing new possibilities in the midst of messy change.

And in hard times, to remember this: *"Look for the signposts."*

Wow — what a timely reminder. To remember, and celebrate, and commemorate His faithfulness.

***KEY #15** – Look for the signposts. Notice and honor what He has done.*

16
Beloved: Story from a Vineyard, Part 1

– FEBRUARY 2019 –

A review, from the first time I came to the vineyard.

It had been a bleak season, months that felt like years, especially in our local community — hard things, heart things. Mike and I were on a "sunshine break" to California, and that day we drove through the Napa Valley; a refreshing drive of lush beauty, a stark contrast to the cold winter back home.

That's when I saw it — field after field of greatly pruned vines, looking stunted and gnarly and decidedly NOT attractive. Between growing seasons. And yet, there were bright golden mustard-plant flowers blooming between all the rows, brightening the otherwise drab scene. They made the fields a photographers' magnet, including this tourist with her little iPhone camera.

But I wondered, *"Why the mustard flowers?"* Sure, they are pretty, but why are they sown? I found out that the mustard plant gives ingredients that protect the vines from invasive pests, and they also bring important nutrients into the soil to boost the coming season. Vital things for this vulnerable time between seasons as well as for the coming crop.

I felt very drawn to this scene. In my own bleak season, I identified with those gnarly cut-back vines, and I prayed further. In my heart I heard, *"These are not just any average fields."* They are special fields, a high-income crop, meticulously looked after and greatly prized. There were fences around certain fields and signs at the front of them proudly displaying the owner's company name — well-known vineyard industry names like Beringer, Kendall-Jackson, Mondavi.

Later, I was still thinking of the fields I'd seen: the cut-back vines, the between-seasons time, the brilliant mustard, the great care given to the fields, and the owner's name on the front fence.

Then in the middle of the scene, I suddenly saw another element — *I saw the figure of Jesus standing in the middle of the field, facing me.* The look on His face was — *oh, my, it was the most tender look I'd ever seen,* as He looked over this field. I also saw the name now at the front fence of this field. The owner's name, beautifully displayed was *"Kingdom Vineyards."*

As I looked again at Jesus, He said, *"The name of this field is Beloved."*

Mic drop. Wow — such a scene, and such a huge encouragement.

His care over His own field, His love for His Beloved. In the middle of any kind of time.

KEY #16 – *Hear our name: Beloved.*
We are His field, His vineyard.

17
Beloved: Story from a Vineyard, Part 2

– JANUARY 2020 –

The second time I came to the vineyard.

Mike and I were on a tour at a notable California vineyard, one with a very beautiful name: "Storybook Mountain Vineyards." This tour date was on the cusp of what we would later know as a time of worldwide pandemic. And *this, the last definitive word I heard*. Probably important! Here is what I wrote after our tour there:

What a great name, Storybook Mountain. *I believe that God was telling us a story: a story of His love.* This vineyard was the most beautiful and well cared for that I'd ever seen. The owner, along with his faithful team of five long-term workers, carefully tended the fields and vines.

I saw healthy organic life there. The tour guide pointed out the fresh green grass, visible at the base of the well-tended vines: a sign of no harsh chemicals, no shortcuts to productivity. It was a clear reminder to me to *check at the ground level for the genuineness of anything* — are signs of "life" real, or artificially produced?

There were fields with two types of growing methods. Fields of single vines, that I called the *Lone Rangers;* and other fields of connected vines with a common drip hose, that I called *Community.* The guide explained that in more recent years, the "community" arrangement had been found to be more productive.

Thinking later about that contrast and the advantage of community — it's true that community can be difficult, and many have been hurt in community; it can be tempting to isolate. I too have been hurt and have needed healing. But healthy community is still vital. By "community" I mean *vital life-giving relationships that go beyond just the surface or mere acquaintance, and that are connected to the true life-source who is Jesus.*

Some visual elements have remained with me: the owner of the vineyard out on his tractor, loving these fields that he had planted; and the dedicated team of five working the field. The love and care that went into this field was so notable. Really meticulous care — every action was done in view of nurturing the vines. And this team knew the field and did all aspects of its care. It was a place of integrity: a place where no workers were brought in who were just hired for the harvest. No, the ones who loved and nurtured the field also did the harvest. I saw a "heads up" note there, to *watch out for any who just want to come in and harvest, but don't know and love the field!*

As Jesus said in John 15:1-5: *"I am the true grapevine, and my Father is the gardener.... you are the branches."* The reminder: I am a branch who is one with the Vine, and I can trust that the

Gardener knows what He's doing. I can trust Him.

After my return from California in early February, I asked the Lord, *"Father, for two years in a row You have spoken to me in pictures and scripture and word all about a vineyard. Why a vineyard, I wonder? Important principles can be gleaned from so many examples: a garden, a house, a mountain, anything in Your creation. So why a vineyard, and why at this time? Father, what are You saying?"*

 Here are some key things that came to mind, to consider:

1. *Relationships, vital connections are very important!* It's important to let God heal any hurts from relationships and walk with a clear heart. And to ask God's wisdom on where and how to connect, and connect in real ways. We need each other.

2. *Maturity and discernment* — a pointer to not fall for just fluff and outward activity, but to look for what is real; to look at the ground level.

3. *Vineyard* — a vineyard, after all, produces wine! Whether you personally do or do not drink wine is not the point; I believe the point is that *wine is a picture of joy!* A picture of sparkling fresh life, God's life in us. It's the very opposite of just dutiful and dry. This picture is not endorsing overdoing any drinking: scripture is clear on that. But the reminder here is that God wants us to ENJOY Him! Relationship with Him is meant to be fresh and sparkling and enjoyable; and His joy is our strength!

4. *The tasting room:* the place where the public is specifically invited in, to taste the finished product of the vineyard. A re-

minder that all this quiet work in the vineyard is not only for us, but is for others to come. That's where they can come and see the product of our life with the King and be drawn to Him as well. As it says in Psalms 34:8, *"Taste and see that the Lord is good!"* Authentic Kingdom life attracts others too.

5. *We are His Beloved.* Especially noted in the view in the first vineyard visit, that field that was so carefully watched over by Him. He is mindful of every aspect that will touch our lives. He is the Owner of our field. And He is the most loving, compassionate, caring, trustworthy Gardener ever. I can trust Him. WE can trust Him.

6. *Again, that wonderful name, Storybook Mountain.* God is telling us a story of His love. It's all about relationship. He carefully tends to those in His field — this is no average field.

It is Kingdom Vineyards, the field named Beloved.

* * *

Looking back on these Vineyard scenes, such notable scenes and thoughts on the eve of pandemic, months that brought so many swift changes. Things that were emphasized here were such pivotal keys to the way forward. At a time when long-term isolation would suddenly be such an easy option, He emphasized our need for each other.

 At a time when fear would so easily predominate, He spoke of trust, in tangible picture language. What a view!

The Owner, the Gardener, the team of five, the sparkling life, the tasting room — all those images at a time when many would search for what is real and life-giving. And the most tenderly-cultivated field named Beloved. Certainly, an amazing picture. And so much truth to take us through any kind of tough time.

***KEY #17** – Trust the most caring Gardener ever.*

TOUGH TIMES CASE STUDY

– SPRING OF 2020, POP QUIZ! –

We can trust Him, the most caring Gardener ever. That was a notable thing to hear, right before a tough test.

To glean pointers on how to make it through tough times, the global pandemic days of 2020 certainly brought a perfect "case study" time to learn from.

Good days to learn — and to add the gathered bits of wisdom to our tool belt.

We had great reminders that peace is not a place — and not a particular peaceful environment. Not a new thing or activity to lean on, as in "this place or activity brings me peace." But the reminder: peace is a Person — Jesus Christ, the Prince of peace. During this time, there were new ideas of how to gather, how to get together — so many new ways. It was also a time of discovering anew the value of "small" — the twos and threes gathering together; such valuable times.

Many points to learn from in those intense, long days called pandemic 2020.

There were many journal entries I wrote during that time, and several are included here. They were like "on the ground reports," with glimpses of how we made it through with heart and focus intact — and how to be propelled forward rather than getting stuck or sidetracked.

A notable time to glean enduring wisdom.

So here to add to the toolbelt is what I am calling:
"The Pandemic Collection."

18
The Pause

– EARLY SPRING OF 2020 –

These words were written in the early, most cloistered weeks of what we all later found was that very long time of pandemic, a time that affected so much for so long. I believe it's helpful to look back and hear of what it was like "on the ground" right then:

What a moment, this giant "Pause" — a great big rest. Like a sabbath; like a hush over the usually bustling city streets and landscape. Yes, I know there are exceptions, very important exceptions like essential services and first-responders in many vital areas. But to the largest extent we've ever seen, the workaday world is on "pause."

So, I asked the Lord, who surely knew this was coming, *"What are you saying? What are YOU doing?"* One thing I've seen, just basic and obvious, is that people are home much more than in former, "normal" times. Families, those in one house, are gathered together. It's like a big "set apart" time.

Such distinctive days — like a future headline might read: "When the Whole World Went Home."

Wait! Does this ever happen? There's the over-used word "unprecedented." Like God is saying to us,

> *"I want to talk to you. Yes, calm down all the outer noise. All. The. Noise. I want to talk to you. Yes, you."*

A time like this can be positive or negative — there are choices for either one. But if we consider that this time could be a great opportunity, and we ask God to please USE this time for good, He could bring great good from this.

There could be opportunity for God to draw together the hearts of parents to their children, and the hearts of children to their parents. There could be healing of hurts, restoring of relationships, and new strength developing in homes as people give God room to do this.

These homes could become houses of hope, homes of healing, even revival centers, all from families coming alive in a new way; all great big possibilities in these strange and trying times! They could be part of a grassroots Holy Spirit movement, touching people in homes around them, and across their neighborhoods — and even cities and regions. It could be transforming.

All possibilities IF we give God room, in this unsettling time; as we simply invite HIM to come in new ways in our ordinary places! No getting all dressed up to "go to church," just BE the church wherever we are. And care about each other, and about others who we don't know yet. Transforming, but starting with one caring person at a time.

And so, I feel a challenge to give God room, in this great big pause; to not squander this time, but to treasure it. Together. I'm reminded of this, Psalm 46:10, *"Be still, and know that I am God."*

And Malachi 4:6, *"...bring together... the hearts of fathers to their children and the hearts of children to their fathers..."*

The Pause — *What will I do with my Pause? What will we do?*

KEY #18 – Use our time well. Lean in and listen.

19
The Power of Small

– SPRING OF 2020 –

Here we are, continuing through these pandemic and quarantine days. Some thoughts were shared last week on an Alaska ministry broadcast I was watching. An observation was shared about gatherings. As they are smaller right now, people can see anew that there's a strength in the twos and threes gathered in His name, as He is in the midst. A reminder that the true strength and authority of the church is in the small.

Those thoughts reminded me of a word from last summer, written here in a previous chapter, that God is *"building brand-new onramps, to meet with you in brand-new ways."* I do believe this is one of the "new onramps" that God is building: discovering afresh the power of small. Some of the new onramps being built involve the church's learning how to do "corporate gathering" in new ways: online services, and worship times in outdoor venues; and smaller meetings on zoom and chat. But this too… the twos and threes: a rediscovery of this, the small.

Matthew 18:20: *"For where two or three are gathered in my name, there am I among them."*

In our world right now, there are so many BIGS: big pandemic, big crises, big confusion over any sense of "normal," big economic problems — it's all so overwhelming. And we think, in the face of all that, what can we do?! I believe that God is reminding us, there is power in the small. Here are three personal reminders, some examples I've had:

1. My small homemade sign I spontaneously put out in the early, most cloistered quarantine time, right here where we live. It said, *"Want Prayer? Call or text (my number)"* We tacked it on a tree at the end of our driveway. This small action led to meeting three neighbors who I'd never known before! And the chance to pray for them!

2. Long ago and far away, a small "nudge" to me, to bring a bouquet of flowers to a particular barista in our Alaskan small town — a woman who I didn't really know, and couldn't easily speak to because of our language barriers. The action of bringing her flowers, which unbeknownst to me was a longed-for answer to her specific prayer that very morning, opened a friendship with her. And soon, friendship with her family, and surprisingly with many others from their ethnic community! That community continued to open to us in many ways through several years! And from what??! From one bouquet of flowers!

3. And today — a thought came to me, to contact one person who's here in our city, far from home for the medical needs of her husband. One person who's alone. The idea was to invite her for dinner. One welcome into our home, one informal BBQ

dinner, conversation and prayer with her; brought her a sense of community and refreshing.

Doing what we can do! The small, the one:

> – ONE sign that offered prayer. And three responses.
> – ONE nudge, one bouquet, for one person, on that one spring day. It opened a friendship and a community.
> – ONE invite today, one drive, one dinner, one prayer, that brought hope.

The power of small. Jesus comes in the midst. It's His power. I believe that Jesus has been dialing us down to the more basic. Seeing individuals — reminding us that *He still calls people one by one*.

It's His power, and His heart.

KEY #19 – Small can be big. Dial-down and see the new view.

20
Lemon Tree in the Marketplace

– MARCH 2020 –

This could actually apply to any time of general anxiety. The Scene: My local supermarket.

All around me was a crowd of intense-looking shoppers. Looking very stressed. Serious faces, super-focused people; stocking up on bottles of water, and toilet paper, and cleaners and sanitizers of various kinds. Serious business. And looking guarded if anyone happened to cough or sneeze near them. Intense scene.

My small cart held some of my usual items: yogurt, salad, tea, coffee. A few cookies, chocolate of course. Then I saw it: a display that was bright and cheerful, with some lemon-yellow décor items. So pretty! And I thought, *"Wow, that looks so summery!"* And at a great discount too! So, I picked out a few branches of faux "lemon tree." I stood up the branches in my cart as I walked along toward the checkout. Many people smiled as I came near them (I could see their smiles as it was not yet a general masking time.) Several people even asked if the lemon tree was real. I noticed the change of mood around me. The shift was really noticeable.

Later, I thought back to that scene and the notable change I'd seen and heard as I walked along with that "lemon tree" through the store. What a distinct difference! "Lemon Tree Power?!" And no kidding, I heard a whisper in my heart, a question to me: *"What do lemons do?"*

Well, I thought, *if I have some cooking odors lingering in my kitchen, I put out a dish of... lemon water. And in many recipes, I can add a refreshing flavor with... lemon zest. And if I have a cold or flu or anything threatening my system, I have hot water and... lemon (usually for me it's lemon essential oil.) When I drink that, it really does kick my immune system into higher gear. And if I want to add cheerfulness to a room, I often add a lemon-yellow color; it brightens the scene and the mood.*

Come to think of it, most "smiley faces" are... lemon yellow. Lemon yellow brings joy, brings hope that "summer's coming!!" So, all told, lemon tree brings refreshing and zest and healing and joy and hope! And I had been wheeling it through my local market.

A further question came to mind, *"Do you know what you carry?"* Hmm... Well, I carry whatever I cultivate on the inside of me. So, it's important what I cultivate, what I welcome in my heart and mind. Because I do affect the atmosphere around me. I carry what I cultivate; all in a little cart that is me. And I am walking routinely through the marketplace!

Especially in very difficult days, like the days and months we are in, I ask myself, *"What do I carry?"* And us, what do we carry? It's really easy in these ongoing challenging days to carry worry, distraction, frustration, anger. And anxiety, so easy to come by. It's much harder, actually counter-cultural, to carry hope; to carry brightness and light; to carry compassion and caring. Things that are so valuable and so sought after.

And yet hope, the kind that endures, is not the kind that I can self-engineer. In my life, I find that my source can't be just me. I run out of steam, and I sink to discouragement all too easily. I need to receive from more than just me — I need to receive from my Father God who gives good gifts, including crucial ones like hope. I welcome Him, and cultivate that counter-cultural hope, like an anchor deep inside. What a great gift: bright lemon-yellow, resilient and genuine!

So, what I learned was that as we walk in our days through the marketplace, each of us affects the atmosphere around us with what we cultivate inside of us! Oh, the things we can learn in our ordinary days!

Life lessons at the market.

KEY #20 – Be a counter-cultural HOPE-carrier! Invest in lemon-yellow!

21
Geranium Wisdom

– SPRING OF 2020 –

My poor geranium — it spent the summer on the front porch and winter in the sunroom, in the same pot for three-plus years. Too long, perhaps? Evidently so!

Its branches are all askew, spindly and awkward-looking; and it's in bad need of a total repotting.

So, do you know what I did? Because I love my plant… I removed the blooms and greatly trimmed back the stems, and then I cut all around it, removing it from its familiar but confined environment. I then planted it in a new pot, with new soil. It may be shocked for a bit, but I'm praying that it prospers in its new "digs."

Do you ever feel like this? Maybe you, and I, were comfortable but cramped, with old soil in need of new nutrients, and we needed trimming and renewing.

Then God started messing with us, taking off blooms (Events? Friendships? Ministries? Favorite roles? Travels?) and then trimmed even further. And we said, *"What do you mean, just go home? And stay there??"*

And then after a while of that home thing, He brought us out into… what??! *"What's a 'new normal?!'"*

Maybe some things were trimmed for a reason. Maybe each of us could be reminded to stop and check with Him before picking up something that He trimmed off. Could be it's something not needed in our new season of prospering.

Here's to a new season and to blooming well!

KEY #21 – Trimming can be good. Welcome the trim and the new "digs."

22
God and The Way Things Are

− JUNE 2020 −

The onramps… the theme that echoed through the months. Even more pertinent as we entered the time of pandemic. So, I wrote of it again… the original thoughts, but updated with the current events and the sense of what was going on here in June of 2020:

A word from one year ago, in June of 2019, has been increasingly highlighted to me:

> *"I am building brand-new onramps, to meet with you in brand-new ways. And I am shaking up your status quo, so you will know I am not contained by your 'familiar.'"*

New onramps — it says why: to meet with God in new ways. So, the new onramps are going somewhere; they are for the purpose of relationship. They are not aimless. It's for relating with God. Onramps go to a highway, heading somewhere. These days are definitely strange days — but not aimless days. They can merge into God-relationship; it's my choice.

And *"shaking up your status quo."* Hmm… status quo, "the way things are." I'd say that's sure been happening! Surely over these recent months, or even days.

Shaking. Rearranging. "The way things are" today is different than "the way things were" in February. Or March. Or last week. Or yesterday.

But what did He say to me last June? About shaking up my status quo: *"…so you will KNOW I am not contained by your 'familiar.'"* So that I will know that He is BIGGER than my boxes, my comfortable, familiar patterns. What I think contains Him. He will not be contained.

So, in the new and strange and unfamiliar landscape, He is God. Way, way bigger than my lens can capture. And He wants me to know Him, wants to draw me close, to be close in with Him.

Isaiah 42:9,13-16: *The "No One Puts This on Their Fridge Scripture."*

It's for us. For now. For today, and onward.

KEY #22 – *God is bigger than our boxes. It's worth it to go with Him.*

23
Prince of Peace

– JUNE 2020 –

So many things were going on, in the on-and-on days of 2020. So much upset, so many factions and divisions, and lots of angst. Many issues, worthy issues, and so many thoughts. But there I was, writing "on the ground and in the day," about this — the Prince of Peace:

In these contentious days, something is on my heart — I hear people asking, "Where is peace? Where is safety?" And they are wondering about this place, or that place. There's a big drawing toward nature: green places, wilderness, people going camping, and hiking, and the list goes on. I dearly love and appreciate many of those things too. I also am going camping, and have been driving along the Inlet quite often.

BUT I'm reminded of a time… it was 1980, and I was upset. At that time, our family lived at Fort Greely, WAY out in the hugely peaceful wilderness of Interior Alaska, a place that we loved. We had lived there for three years. But now we were being transferred, by the US Army, to the east coast, Washington DC area — the "big city," where we clearly did NOT want to move! Our mental picture was of nothing but concrete, a crowded, noisy, tension-filled arena.

Into this mental picture and my anxious heart entered God, interrupting my thoughts with this:

> *"If I am the Prince of Peace only in the country, only in Alaska, then I am most certainly NOT the Prince of Peace. I need to show you, I am the Prince of Peace wherever I send you. I am the God of the City as well."*

He did show us this, even over our protests. In our three years of living there in the DC area, He showed us amazing grace and miraculous provision. He showed us wonderful church family and good friends and beauty. And yes, He showed us there were many godly, wonderful things going on, right there in the city. We had friends in the Senate and the White House who were dynamic praying people, and many lives were being touched. Right there. In. The. City.

Those words from 1980 remind me today that *peace is not a place*. Peace is not a particular peaceful scene. It's ours wherever He sends us. Because *peace is a Person — Jesus, the Prince of Peace*.

Jesus — Prince of Peace / Address — Anywhere.

KEY #23 – *Remember, peace is a Person, anywhere He leads.*

24
Change the Atmosphere

– AUGUST 2020 –

As the year continued, or more like dragged on, many gatherings were cancelled, and many churches remained closed or had services greatly altered out of caution. Personal encouragement was even more crucial than in former days — days that we weren't sure would ever come back. There was so much uncertainty. Unique times, with unique ideas to help us come through. Here is one such thought that came to me at that time:

In the midst of strange days, and with a sense of gloom here in the air, what comes to mind is the value of brave moments, to *"just worship."*

That's right, just us! Each of us, separate from any church community gathering, or not gathering. Just EACH of us begin to sing and worship God.

So, here's the picture: *to just go out on our front porches, or back decks, or open our windows if that is what we've got!*

And DO the action spoken of in Psalm 96:1: *"Sing a new song to the Lord! Let the whole earth sing to the Lord!"* The whole earth — wow, that includes us!

Radical, right?! Yes, it is! And personally, it's not that I sing well — I do not. And maybe that porch might need a Bluetooth speaker or boom box melody or guitar player to help. And there's no need to be obnoxiously loud. But each of us could just begin to sing, begin to worship. And realize that when we do this, we change the atmosphere!

So ok, I did it. Evening time, I went out to my back deck. Just me. No Bluetooth or anything. I just quietly began to sing. A simple song from decades ago came to mind, *"Gracious Father, gracious Father, we're so glad to be Your children, gracious Father…"*

As I continued to sing, a new verse came with it, so I sang, *"O dear Daddy, O dear Daddy, I'm so blessed to be Your daughter, O dear Daddy…"*

All of a sudden, just quietly in that evening moment, God surprised me — He healed something in me. An emotional healing, so many layers down; a long-standing need that I wasn't even asking about. He even explained to me why it was so deep. *O dear Daddy…* it was like He just HANDED it to me, like *"Here, honey — have some healing."*

No striving, no strain, just enjoying Him. And the atmosphere changes. And He even surprises us with sweet gifts straight from Him. And even wider changes can happen in the atmosphere around us. Gloom lifts off and is replaced with His light and sunshine.

Let's do it. Want to change it up? It's radical and fun, and it's free! And it's just like Him to use little things like this!

He changes atmospheres ALL the TIME.

KEY #24 – Release our voices in worship, and shift the atmosphere!

25
Get the Boats Ready

– NOVEMBER 2020 –

We were visiting recently at a family home when a beautiful painting on their wall caught my attention. As I looked into the scene portrayed, it meant even more to me than the beauty of the painting itself…

Portrayed there in skillful strokes were two boats. And I thought, *"Wow! Look at those magnificent boats!"* Built tough, of sturdy wood, deep enough for a big catch. But with a raised silver edge on the hull that seemed almost touchable. The silver was soft and buffed-looking, like it had been through a refining. Then I heard clearly to my heart, *"Get the boats ready."* Get them ready, for a lot of fish. A whole lot.

But in the scene pictured, there was not only one boat, but two. A main boat and a backup. It reminded me of the story in Luke 5, when the disciples had been fishing but catching nothing. Then they let down their nets again, at Jesus' timing and word. When they did that, they caught such a huge number of fish that they couldn't handle it! They needed to signal to their partners in another boat, asking for them to come and help. Yes, they had partners! And they could've used yet another boat, because there were so many fish.

The very picture of revival. We've prayed for it. But we've envisioned it coming in our neat predictable boxes, our familiar borders, and our little boat. But then… 2020. And months of change and inconvenience and general stress. And "church," we've been reminded by now, is the people, not the building. Oh, some are meeting in buildings, but also in the new ways we've talked about. "The church" is gathering in parking lots, city squares, parks, and beaches. And in virtual gatherings and creative meetups. The church is expanding its footprint in all these ways. The church is "out on the water."

And in the middle of it all, here comes Jesus, walking on the water.

And the hungry, the thirsty, the radical, the prodigal, the stranger, the confused, the scared, both young and old, are coming. They're coming Home.

In such a time as this, what is needed? WE are needed.

Us, "fishers of men," with boats ready, out on the water. Yes, us! Not preoccupied with our own angst about messiness and inconvenience, but looking out for others and their needs. Casting the nets. Caring and reaching out.

And partners: yes, HAVING partners, networking with others who are trustworthy. Key word, trustworthy. But having real connection with those trustworthy ones, walking in unity and strength, despite perhaps having different ways or styles. Able and ready to be the backup for each other. Team fishing. These are those kinds of days!

All to be ready for the ones coming — and remembering the word, *"Get the boats ready!"*

KEY #25 – Live ready to reach out. Connect with trustworthy partners.

26
Agent 99 vs Chaos

– NOVEMBER 2020 –

Months that had been difficult continued in that vein. And in the late fall timeframe, the former intensity became intensity in ALL CAPS!! Not only politically, but our culture in general became much more adversarial. I wrote the following at that time:

I woke up with a dream. I don't generally dream; I do see pictures in prayer, but when I sleep, I sleep. This was an unusual dream — it was of a TV show, a very old one. One that I hadn't thought of for many years. And no, I didn't even know there's apparently a current version of it. The show was called "Get Smart." It was a comedy, with really corny humor that we loved. The chief characters were Agent Maxwell Smart (who was not smart at all) and his partner, a woman called "Agent 99" — she was the actually smart one! And the enemy was a set of goofy characters, always named "Chaos." So that was my whole dream, this reminder of the main characters, and especially their names, highlighting Agent 99 and Chaos. Goofy, huh? Except that the image of all this remained, and increased in emphasis.

I realize this dream came in a highly adversarial and political season, and tension was high. But the dream went way beyond anything political.

I looked up the definition of "chaos" — it means *"utter confusion and disorder."* Sounds like a description of activity by the enemy of our souls: that one who is never for us, but is always aimed at our destruction. His activity, chaos, is aimed at our hearts. No matter what kind of "chaos" is going on around us, the target is us.

I want to underline that — I believe that *"chaos" aims at our hearts*. No matter what the situation, WE are the target. The aim of "chaos" is adversarial, wanting to cause breaks in relationships, especially in our relationship with our dear Father God. Chaos is aiming at us.

Further, I asked God, *"What is this Agent 99? And who is that?"* By the way, that very morning the "9" was highlighted for us here in Alaska with nine earthquakes in our region, a couple of them really notable! *"Ok, ok,"* I thought, *"so there's something about nine!"* So, I looked up Psalm 99 — which as it turns out has nine power-packed verses.

Here is Psalm 99:1 (NLT):

> *"The LORD is king! Let the nations tremble! He sits on His throne between the cherubim. Let the whole earth quake!"*

And it goes on, all nine verses about the King, and His character of holiness; and that He loves justice and fairness, and acts in righteousness. His character, His heart. He is the real King, above any earthly ruler. Wow.

I believe the dream I had points to the King, His character and His heart. The King came to us in the person of the Lord Jesus Christ. I believe that He, and all who surrender their hearts to this LORD, who is the King — that we, together, are Agent 99.

As we walk in alignment with the King, we counter chaos, and the King wins. No matter how crazy the world around us gets, the lifestyle of the King gets to rule; and love rather than fear wins the day.

So, here's a pledge for our hearts: *No matter how sideways anything gets, if we choose to walk in step with the King, His resilient love will rule in our hearts. And we will not be ruled by chaos. Sorry, chaos, you do not win. The King wins — every time.*

In the middle of hard times: remember who we are, sons and daughters of the King; and align with His plan.

The King wins — and chaos does not.

KEY #26 – Align with the King and counter chaos. Be ON Team 99!

27
Receiving

— DECEMBER 2020 —

In the middle of holiday times, or *any* intense time, there are so many needs. Givers do just that: they give, in so many ways. But what has come to mind lately is the importance, especially for givers, to receive. Yes, the word is *receive* — often a difficult thing for givers to do.

In my own heart, I've been hearing this, *"Come, gather in, children — I have gifts for you. This is a time to receive. Yes, gifts for YOU! There will be a time to come when you will give, even these same things, to others. But right now, it's time for you to receive."*

Some gifts came to mind, found in Isaiah 32:1-2:

> *"Behold, a king will reign in righteousness, and princes* [sons and daughters of the king] *will rule in justice. Each will be like a hiding place from the wind, a shelter from the storm, like streams of water in a dry place, like the shade of a great rock in a weary land."*

As I look through these verses, I think of the days we're in. Hmm... wind, storm, dry place, weary land... check! Yes, we're there. And the needs are many. Givers really know that and are inclined to give to many of those needs. Often, that is me too. But the emphasis in this time — is about intentionally receiving. So, for me, I look to do this too. To receive these specific things from that passage in Isaiah 32:

1. The King — I receive His reigning in righteousness in me. He is King and I am not.

2. Princes — I receive that I am a daughter of the King and I have authority; and that authority is from His rule.

3. Hiding place — I come into the hidden place, the protected place, close with Him.

4. Shelter — I receive that in this storm-filled time, He is my covering, my safe place.

5. Streams of water — I receive His refreshing in these dry-feeling days; I drink in of His presence and fill up with Him!

6. Shadow of a great rock — The only way to be in His shadow is to be right next to Him, my mighty rock, shaded and covered.

Also, the reminder is that there will be a time to give of these same things to others. There will be a time to BE that safe place, that refreshing one.

Father, I thank You that You invite me to come into You, in what You know is good timing and for my good. I'm saying "Yes!" And I determine to come in now and receive Your gifts.

Readers, I invite you too to come on in and receive. God gives *great* gifts! Nothing frivolous here; every gift is a treasure.

KEY #27 – *Especially for givers, there's a time to receive.*

28
Dichotomies

– JANUARY 2021 –

These are dark days — with so much uncertainty in our own hearts and in the world around us.
But — God is building an army that will stand. And He's equipping us more and more each day.

Evil seems to be triumphing.
But — Many are searching for an anchor in these tumultuous times.

Division, strife, misunderstanding and offense abound.
But — God is weaving together diverse streams of those listening to and responding to Him.

Days of despair and depression in many.
But — Days of expansion and creativity also in many.

Days of hatred and division.
But — Days too of unity and strength.

And I hear God saying, *"Come up here with Me — I will show you how to walk in these days in My perspective, in humility that walks with others, and weaves together with others, combining different giftings and strengths."*

Days of *"Get the boats ready"* (no, not the Ark to sail away!) but fishing boats mentioned earlier, sturdy ones. Because many fish will be coming in, even right in the middle of messy days — and this is TEAM fishing!

There are so many details we don't know yet; we don't know how these dicey days are going to all shake out. But one thing we know:

> *"Father, You have built an army and are continuing to equip us and help us with teamwork. This is a spiritual army, under Your direction, that will stand."*

Our enemy — is definitely NOT people, but principalities and powers, and spiritual wickedness in the spiritual realm. (See Ephesians 6.) God's army is strong, and working together, spanning across the continent and around the world. *It's phenomenal what YOU, God, are doing!*

Father, thank You! We submit to You, in what YOU are building! We yield to Your strength.

KEY #28 – *See His view, and discern the contrasts.*

29
Real News

– WINTER OF 2021 –

I woke up with a picture and narrative of the average "evening news" model.

It reminded me that each night, the program ties a succinct little package, and presents itself as the real factual "news." But the neatly-wrapped package includes quite a lot of fear, delivered each day to the average viewer. Much of it alarming, more things to be afraid of, incomplete "factual" reports, and much of it politically slanted.

Some news is real. Just not all. The average version is delivered in a fear-based tone. Because news is business, and advertising, a part of business — and the sensational sells. Sad truth.

All this, delivered daily. As such, it can form a mindset. Every. Day.

Fear can also manipulate people and lead them as if in herds to an intended direction.

So, should we hide our heads in the sand and avoid real reports of real events? No. Really, absolutely NO. There's value in making the effort to look up a variety of news sources, and to also check *their* sources.

Real news is important. And beyond that, some news is timeless. Like Psalm 46, that informs us of Who is actually in charge. As in verse 10 of that Psalm: *"Be still and know that I am God."* It tells us that because of that reality, we do not need to fear.

Here's another "real news" flash — this scripture, Psalm 29, that lets us know that His voice is far above the noise of our days.

Psalm 29:3-11:

> *"The voice of the Lord is over the waters;*
> *the God of glory thunders, the Lord, over many waters.*
> *The voice of the Lord is powerful;*
> *the voice of the Lord is full of majesty.*
>
> *The voice of the Lord breaks the cedars;*
> *the Lord breaks the cedars of Lebanon.*
> *He makes Lebanon to skip like a calf,*
> *and Sirion like a young wild ox.*
> *The voice of the Lord flashes forth flames of fire.*
>
> *The voice of the Lord shakes the wilderness;*
> *the Lord shakes the wilderness of Kadesh.*
> *The voice of the Lord makes the deer give birth [or, 'makes the oaks shake']*
> *and strips the forests bare, and in his temple all cry 'Glory!'*

The Lord sits enthroned over the flood;
the Lord sits enthroned as king forever.
May the Lord give strength to his people!
May the Lord bless his people with peace!"

And I especially love The Passion Translation of verse 10: "Above the furious flood, the Enthroned One reigns, the King-God rules with eternity at his side."

Wow — "Above the furious flood, the Enthroned One reigns..."

Good to remember — our real news is from our real Father. His message to us is not just to "stay safe," but He keeps, and leads, and shows us what is truly important.

Real news for our real days.

KEY #29 – *Feed on real timeless truth! Remember Who is really ruling.*

30
At the Beach

– MARCH 2021 –

Back at our favorite vacation place in Mexico.

I was at the beach today. It has been two years — two long years for us and for the whole world, since I last walked on this beloved beach. After all we'd been through, it was comforting to walk at this familiar place. And then I saw the rocks.

This place, the beloved landscape, looked different. Like the beach had somehow shifted. There used to be a large expanse of smooth sand beach. Now there were many rock formations, and less sand on this beach. What happened??

Twenty-four months. That's it. Twenty-four months happened. Especially these last twelve. Months when they too had been through the downturn. The extended time when people couldn't come. And the resort, reduced to minimal staffing. Not many people to take care of a beach. Times of tumult and hardship. They too had seen a very adverse environment.

And the storms came, and the winds blew, and the waves crashed upon the beach. And much sand was washed away, revealing the rock beneath.

Adversity — hard days and then months, revealed that rock.

Looking at this, I could see the result of what we ALL had been through. The earth itself gave witness. Adversity — and what it reveals. Adversity reveals our bedrock. Sturdy, steady bedrock; it was there all along — HE was there all along. We could stand on Him.

So, this question comes to mind: *"What am I standing on? What are you standing on?"* Standing on the Rock, or a sand castle? Something that will hold, or something that will wash away? He, Jesus, is the Rock. The only One. He is the One safe to stand on, safe to build our lives and our homes on, and to have a steady future on.

What a reminder, at this beach. A reminder that it's time to check.

* * *

You can read about it in Matthew 7:24-27:

> *House on rock / storms come -> House stands.*
> *House on sand / storms come -> House falls.*

Notice, storms come to both. That's a given. But the end result: that's where we see the big difference!

This view of the beach gives an invitation to each of us: to check our grounding. And to trade in any ways of building on sand castles, for building on true Rock.

He takes trade-ins all the time, and He gives the real thing.

"Storms Happen" — a good time to check for bedrock is now.

KEY #30 – Storm-proofing.
Rock is solid! Sturdy in adversity.

31
The Key of Peace

- JUNE 2021 -

PEACE — A question came to me, *"Do you know how big Peace is?"*

> Colossians 3:15: *"Let the peace of Christ rule in your hearts…"*

In the middle of a difficult time, this came to mind: the peace of Christ is STRONG peace. Not wimpy, not circumstantial, not the kind that flits away at the first sign of trouble. No, it is slogging-through-the-trenches peace. The kind that doesn't leave when everything in the world, or my personal world or yours, is upset.

This kind of peace counters evil, and oppression, and all that would try to squash and overcome us. The kind that's spoken of in Romans 16:20: *"The God of peace will soon CRUSH satan under your feet."* That's strong peace! Fighting evil, and fighting it through us! (For instance, I will not capitalize the name of our enemy.)

It's also the kind of peace that guards us on the inside, in our thoughts and motivations. As is spoken of here in Philippians 4:7:

> *"And the peace of God, which surpasses all understanding, will guard your hearts and minds in Christ Jesus."*

And a reminder back in that beginning verse of Colossians 3:15: *"LET the peace of Christ rule in your hearts…"* We have the turnkey. We can let (allow) this peace to rule, or not. We can allow this peace to not only dwell, to live there in our hearts, but to actually RULE — to be the umpire, and call the shots.

The verse goes on: *"…to which you are called…"* Wow, having peace that rules is not just OUR desire, but HIS calling for us. So, we are not being presumptuous. We are designed for peace!

The verse concludes with three words. *"And be thankful."* Three. Little. Words. How hard could it be??! Like God is saying to us, *"…and oh, by the way, be thankful."* And yet, it's so easy to be grumbly and ungrateful, anything but thankful.

One thing comes to mind just now. There's something about being thankful that is humbling. Being the recipient of grace, not the owner. Like we are not "all that," but HE is. Something about being thankful maintains our hearts in a receptive openness.

And apparently, being thankful is connected to letting the peace of Christ rule.

> *Thankful heart / peace rules.*
> *Ungrateful heart / chaos rules.*

"And be thankful." Keep an open, receptive heart.

It's not easy, but we have the turnkey. We are designed for peace. It sure sounds worth it.

KEY #31 – *Use the turnkey and let His strong peace rule.*

32
Principles of Refreshing

– SUMMER 2021 –

In the middle of difficult times that seem long, how important is refreshing?

The Bible speaks of people and settings that bring refreshing: we've looked at Isaiah 32:2, that mentions people who would be *"...like streams of water in a dry place."* And Romans 15 speaks about refreshing when life-giving friends have time together.

Refreshing. It sounds so simple. I found myself in need of this refreshing, after some particularly stretching months. And God highlighted to me several basic actions to do that would help.

The first was for my body — things like:

1. Breathe — and I thought, *"Really, breathe??!"* That's awfully basic! And I heard in my heart, *"Yes, breathe — you don't realize it, but when you're stressed, your breathing is shallow. So yes, breathe — deeply."*

2. Drink — pure water. Again, so basic! And for added benefit, it could be water with fresh or essential oil lemon! So, His advice to me, *"Drink up!"*

3. Eat — real food. The whole phrase to me was to *"eat food that your body can recognize as real."* So, whole natural foods, foods without artificial ingredients. And the instruction to ENJOY those foods! To sit down and take the time to taste and enjoy, and *savor the flavor!* To thank Him for the food, and eat, not with guilt but with gratefulness.

4. Rest — relax! A reminder to me that naps are good! And so is sleep at night, worth preparing well for it. Good preparations like a dial-down, non-techy time before bed, and setting a restful environment for sleep.

5. Exercise — admittedly my weakest area. But the idea is to do this not in a begrudging sense of duty but as a gift.

6. Physical touch — hugs are healthy! And massage, really beneficial too.

7. Blessing — a reminder to thank Him for the gift of life. And to be thankful for and bless, and not curse, my body.

For my soul — an assortment of ideas:
1. Do something simple — something tactile, non-techy. Paint, color, sculpt. Realize the value of touching things that are natural and real. Real paper book. Real fabric.

2. Laugh — what a simple reminder, God wants me to laugh! Proverbs 17:22 says it's like medicine! Vitamins for my soul. Deep-down, belly laughter — it's good for me!

3. Simplify personal environment — I streamlined one very doable area. Cleared one counter. It made a visual difference — and even that little thing felt good!

4. Change colors — this small shift can bring a fresh tone to a room or a home. How wonderful that God has made me so complex, I can respond to my environment like that!

5. Community — when I get together with uplifting people, I too am affected. Their encouragement is contagious! They are vital connections. And when I encourage someone else, I too am uplifted.

Refreshing for the core of me, for my spirit:
1. Be still, wait on Him, and sense the Presence of the original Refresher. And He reminds me to receive from Him, His peace.

2. Worship Him — turn on the worship music; sing, or do whatever helps me to turn my eyes to Him and above situations — turn to the King.

3. Pray in the Spirit, as led by Him, and give Him my cares and worries, anything that concerns me, with the assurance that He wants to hear my heart.

4. Take communion often, even daily — gather the elements, and receive them thoughtfully. Thank God for the gift of life and for the sacrifice He gave so that I can live whole in Him.

I was reminded of so many basic concepts, for me to not only think about but to DO. Such basic things can actually affect my days — especially in times of coming through or recovering from challenging days or months.

These basic ideas helped a lot — they were much more important than I had thought. What a huge gift, refreshing! It is why I am sharing them here with you as well. Go for it!

Refreshing — it's really vital to long-term, enduring strength.

KEY #32 – Don't overlook simple. Breathers are vital for endurance.

33
Orphan

– FALL OF 2021 –

Who can heal the human heart, the core memories, the inner motivations? Only the God who made us. And who needs healing? People may think that only those with hugely dysfunctional backgrounds need healing, or ones who are young, or who are young in this walk of faith.

But He is touching ones who have walked with God for many years, and He's healing at deeper levels than ever before — including touching ones like me, one who had a fairly functional "normal" background. For all of us have been "raised by humans" — and humans make mistakes! In my case, I was born during a time of strain in the early years of my immediate family. And in the middle of it all, I felt unwanted. Yes, even in a normal home there can be gaps!

To grow in emotional health, we can receive teachings and learn better patterns of living and thinking. We can have sessions with many kinds of caring professionals and learn better coping skills. Those things can be highly valuable. But I believe that only the God who made us can heal us from the core deep inside.

Quite recently, God talked with me about something He called "*orphan.*" Orphan is one who doesn't know his/her Daddy, so (in my case, "she") orphan also does not know who she is. Her life is spent in striving to BE someone, to be worthwhile and valuable. I began to see different expressions of this core need.

This inner striving shows up in a variety of ways in different settings. In school or work: it could be overachieving, or striving for recognition; or conversely, giving up. In social circles: the same striving, and gravitating toward whatever is the prominent "in-crowd," whether pro- or anti-social crowd. In family circles: it could be competition, comparison, the need to win; or conversely, withdrawing. So, whether in school, work, social circle, family, community or ministry, the main characteristics are basically the same — competition, comparison, a need for recognition and to appear to be a "winner." Or again, there can be the opposite direction, giving up and withdrawing.

In ministry circles, where I was shown the most detail, characteristics are the same, but because those characteristics put on a more "spiritual" cover, they can be more difficult to spot. But they could involve reliance on roles or titles of perceived importance, or the need to exhibit a style or sound similar to whoever is admired in the particular circle. In prophetic circles, there could be adding length or emphasis or volume to something shared, in order to sound like whichever ones are admired. Mainly, going beyond what is natural (each person has their own genuine "natural") — or conversely, holding back, feeling that a simple word is, well, "too simple," or that it would not "measure up." (The term 'measure up' is a clue to comparison, which the Bible says is never wise.) (2 Corinthians 10:12)

Bottom line — striving, in whatever arena, is exhausting! Striving leads to exhaustion which can lead to quitting. As I saw the various expressions of orphan, I realized that some of those patterns were in me. So, I asked God to go to the root of any orphan expressions in me.

How does God heal pervasive patterns, deeply rooted in the personality? He goes to the core. (He knows where it is!) And He then heals it from there. The ways and moments of Him doing that are as unique as each of us. For me, He surprised me with a scene, a glimpse. I had been in some healing prayer times and sessions in the past, and during those times I had seen Jesus being present back at my moment of birth and embracing me; saying, *"I rejoiced on the day you were born!"* And that glimpse had been beautiful and had been very healing at some levels. But this time, in a surprise moment, I saw a new glimpse of my way-back-when self, not as a just-birthed infant but as a little girl, three or four years old. And in the scene, my "adult me" embraced my "little girl me." I felt God's presence so strongly, and I said to her, *"Barbi Lynne, you are so cute! With bright blue eyes!"* And I fully embraced her.

I thought, *"Wow, what happened there?!! Receiving / embracing of self — from self."* I'd NEVER seen that before! And deep on the inside of me, I felt like a switch was turned from off to ON. And I thought, *"Wow, a psychologist would likely call this something important!"* Maybe "Integration?" Something, certainly, that counters dissonance and inner conflictedness. I call it *Healing at the CORE of Orphan*. I call it Peace / Shalom — nothing broken, nothing missing. Real wholeness.

As this healing moment continued, I also saw myself, even at that young age, with many gifts that God had fitted me with, gifts that were a part of the real me. I saw that loving and caring were really me (at that age, it was caring about puppies and dollies) — and coloring was something I already loved! (I still do!) And I saw that later, I greatly loved a diversity of cultures. I saw that those things were a part of me, not artificially added. Truly me. This healing unlocked a sense of joy and freedom deep inside. The ways of healing are so unique. But when God does it, there are the hallmarks of His presence and freedom!

God not only healed at the core, but He also led me in wisdom for how to proceed in emotional health. The whole process, to be guarded by peace. He reminded me of John 14:27 (NLT): *"I am leaving you with a gift — peace of mind and heart. And the peace I give is a gift the world cannot give. So don't be troubled or afraid."*

His peace, the guardian. That steady peace is important, because *deep-down healing does get attacked.* Also important is ammunition for the road ahead.

My ammo was scripture. He showed me Isaiah 61:7:

> *"Instead of your shame there shall be a double portion; instead of dishonor they shall rejoice in their lot; therefore, in their land they shall possess a double portion; they shall have everlasting joy."*

He also showed me Isaiah 62:4:

> *"You shall no more be termed Forsaken, and your land shall no more be termed Desolate, but you shall be called*

My Delight is in Her, and your land Married, for the Lord delights in you, and your land shall be married."

On the basis of those scriptures, here's what I received to declare, and displace the old with the new:

1. I trade in shame and dishonor; I receive double portion, and rejoicing.

2. I trade in brokenness; I receive deep-down healing.

3. I trade in fear; I receive freedom, and a voice to speak what You give me to speak; no more, and no less.

4. I trade in unwanted; I receive wanted, and the place You open for me at the table; I can simply look for what You open, and sit there.

5. I trade in rejection; I receive full embrace: from You, Father, and from community, from family, and from myself, from me.

6. I trade in downcast; I receive joy and rejoicing!

7. I receive my name: Beloved. And I receive (you could insert your name here) — but for me, I receive Barbi Lynne (Barbi = close one; Lynne = refreshing pool.)

8. I receive (from Isaiah 62) my name is Bride, Redeemed, Delight, Sought out (the opposite of orphan.)

9. I receive my place to stand with You.

* * *

Healing that is this deep can also connect with physical healing, and especially healing of any autoimmune disease — which by definition, is *the body fighting itself and its own natural immune response;* and so, can be linked with internal dissonance and conflictedness. I am not a medical professional; I am, however, recognizing the linkages between soul and body. Because my spirit, soul and body are connected! *So, Father, I am believing You for the outworking of inner freedom that You bring!* This is an adventure, to be continued!

What huge things God is doing! There has been a pervasive sense of freedom in me since this recent healing time. Healing that is so deep down. At the place of self-image and motivations. I believe it is KEY to walking steadily, for each of us through all our days, whether ordinary or extraordinarily difficult days.

He is the Master Healer.

KEY #33 – *Simply receive from the Master Healer*

34
Blaze Orange Dream

– 2021 & 2022 –

Dreaming, or remembering a dream, is unusual for me; and this dream was, well, quite unusual.

It was nighttime in the dream, a very dark night. And the scene was in a treed area in my front yard. My front yard is not large, but there's a small patch of trees we jokingly call our "100-acre wood." One tree is nearest the driveway, a tall tree, that I call my "sentinel tree." So, in the dream, high up in the sentinel tree was a bird — an extremely vivid orange, what I would call "blaze orange." It was totally that blaze orange color, except for a luminous bright blue on the top side of its wings. The bird was fairly large, and it looked like a caricature, as if from a children's cartoon movie. It lived there in the sentinel tree — it wasn't caged or kept there, but I sensed it was just "pleased to live there." And it was a happy bird!

In the patch of woods near it, in the dream there was another animal, a cow. It was a wide cow, beefy looking, and it was black, with shiny super-clean wavy black hair on its hide. It was not a calf, but a full-grown cow. It was not fenced or tied there, but "pleased to live there." It was a happy cow! And despite the very dark night scene, there was no sense of fear or foreboding. There was one phrase, the only phrase I heard, *"Don't be afraid."*

I woke up and thought *"Wut? What?! What a strange dream!"* But the dream continued to be on my heart, and my sense increased about what it means. So here goes:

1. *Bird in the sentinel tree* — Sentinel, watchman, guardian; being right next to the driveway, it was watching over all comings and goings in and out of our home.

2. *Blaze orange* — Reminded me of the pillar of fire that God sent to guide Israel in nighttime in the wilderness; I was also reminded of the term "the fiery presence of God." So, the impression was of being guarded, watched over, by His fiery presence.

3. *Driveway* — Gateway, access point — the picture of God guarding over the gateway, the access point to our home. And screening carefully whatever would try to get through, to touch us or our home.

4. *Luminous bright blue on the top of wings* — Emphasized the heavenly; referring to His Spirit; confirming that this was about God's own presence.

5. *The bird lives there* — Not constrained, but "pleased to live there." So good!

6. *Cow in the woods* — Wide cow, not skinny, not a calf — reminded me of provision, resource. Shiny-clean wavy hair — not dusty like in a feedlot. Clean, as contrasted with "unclean;" and like the bird, this cow was not fenced, but "pleased to live there."

And in reference to the cow, I was also reminded of the word "Goshen." When the Israelites were in Egypt, they lived in Goshen. Plagues came upon cows in Egypt but not upon cows in Goshen, as it says that *God made a distinction between the two.* (Exodus 9)

Another place where the Bible talks of a distinction being made is at the end of the Old Testament, in the book of Malachi. In contrast to previous verses of rebuke, there is this in Malachi 3:17-18:

> "'They shall be mine,' says the Lord of hosts, 'in the day when I make up my treasured possession; and I will spare them as a man spares his son who serves him. Then once more you shall see the distinction between the righteous and the wicked, between one who serves God and one who does not serve him.'"

The phrase that came to mind when thinking through this dream was "the home of the righteous." And it's one reason I'm relating this dream here. Because although this was my yard, and I do receive these promises personally, I don't believe the promises in this dream are just for my yard and home. It's for the "home of the righteous." Notice, it's not "home of the perfect." The home of the righteous is the home of those who have received the MERCY of the Father in the person of Jesus

Christ — that's *"the home of the righteous."* Equal opportunity offer here!

And that bird: so distinctive. Blaze orange, the fiery presence — and also the color of JOY! The joy of the Lord is our strength! It was also an image of BEAUTY — bright and fluffy beauty! The animals in this dream were at a place in our yard that is normally visible to me from my kitchen window, like a visible assurance. And yet the scene is shielded from a street view, so it is not well seen by others.

And again, the emphasis — even though the scene was a VERY dark night, the word, *"Don't be afraid,"* is still echoing to me. Putting this together, I believe this dream is a promise being given to believers in the Lord Jesus Christ, about our homes and our families. It is pointing to this: that even in the midst of very dark days, and perhaps darker days coming, it's a promise of guardianship and protection over the gateways to our homes, and over all comings and goings. And for resource and provision — clean provision, not dirt and sweat and stress; abundant provision; from God's blessing, who is pleased to live there; and a reminder that the joy of the Lord is our strength.

I am sharing this dream because the promises expressed are valuable for each of us to receive, and actually to declare over ourselves and over our homes and families. I believe it is timely. And I may even commemorate it in some way, like with a blaze-orange painted rock. I think I will put that by my sentinel tree!

God is SO good — He gives vivid, wild dreams to His loved ones, His treasures. He even calls us by these terms, because He IS that good! Bright days, dark days, darker days, He's got us in His hands. What an amazing God, the Giver of dreams. No matter what kind of days, His promises are bright with hope that is real!

***KEY #34** – Receive His bright promises! KNOW His guardianship and provision.*

35
The Role of Joy

– SUMMER OF 2022 –

The role of Joy. I've been thinking of its importance, especially to the warriors, ones coming through hard things, battle-scarred but persevering. The things we battle are serious. And these days are intense! The recurring thought is about the joy of the Lord, our strength — and of joy being part of the strategy of walking through long-term battles.

Really valuable things — fun and joy. The gift of wonder, and lightness, and laughter. A phrase that came to mind recently, *"What if FUN is not an 'interruption' on the way to doing the IMPORTANT stuff?"* What if it's part of our weaponry, something that reminds us that God is in charge?

So many things in these days are serious. "Lightening up" may be needed for balance!

Again, I've thought of the dream I had last year about this time, that I just described here. A very dark night — in fact an extreme, inky-black dark night. And yet… the images in this dream, symbols of serious subjects, God's vigilant guardianship and abundant provision, were images that looked like cartoons, like caricatures! Bright, outlandish colors, cartoonish characters.

He could've used much more heavy and formidable symbols! But instead, He showed something light, something really "outta the box," colorful and wild!

Why?? And He gave a couple clues — about *"Goshen,"* and about *"the home of the righteous."* Clues that led me to the books of Exodus and Malachi — much like a treasure hunt!

He not only gave clues, but the images themselves were a huge contrast to the inky black night. Those bright images tell me even now, that *He is not worried about the scene He is describing!*

Like He is pointing to, *"I've got this! Why not laugh?!"*

All of these things, clues that the joy of the Lord really IS our strength! Even in serious days — maybe ESPECIALLY in serious days!

So today, I pray for the warriors, ones who may feel nearly crushed by ongoing battle. *Thank You Father, that Your view is of winning, and laughter is a real weapon!*

Father, I pray, fill up each of us with Your joy, and Your perspective. Fill our hearts with Your joy! Fill us with a sense of wonder. And we thank You even now for Your amazing guardianship and provision! Hallelujah! Thank You that YOU reign!

Difficult days, intense wearying battles?

Remember the weapon of joy, our strength. HE is in charge.

KEY #35 – *Remember that Joy is a weapon — it's our strength!*

36
Sturdy / Steady House and Life

– JULY 2022 –

I talked with a young friend the other night, about foundations. One of our quips was this: "Before you build your house (or life) check on foundation — for instance, that you HAVE one. One that will stand." Since then, I have had further thoughts about this subject. Ideas about foundation: and how important that good foundation is to a house, and especially to a life.

Matthew 7:24-27 refers to this, about a house built on rock versus a house built on sand — and shows exactly how each worked out!

To build a steady life — like the bedrock talked about earlier in "At the Beach" — a sturdy foundation is extremely important. Well-founded. So, the thought is, check what the foundation is based on: Rock, especially THE Rock, who is Jesus Christ. Or on sand: the vagaries of culture, and handy little bits of opinion.

So, the admonition is to build on what is solid, on what is forever-real.

Another word about this came to me later: *"You're going to need a 'moat' around your house and your life."* A complete surround. Long ago, a moat was a deep, wide ditch, usually full of water, that surrounded castles and other fortified structures. It helped in defense of the castle. This current word gave that thought, but also added this, *"The best moat is the blood of Jesus Christ."* Different from just water, it's about His Life surrounding mine. Not just a little bit, or a little dab, which is just religion — but completely surrounding my house and life. We're talking SURROUNDED — by the blood of Jesus, the Christ.

One more phrase followed: *"...and you'll need a good functioning drawbridge."* Again, in days of long ago, spanning across that moat to the castle, was a drawbridge. Its function was to let in some things and keep out others. So, the thought is, *it's important what I let into my house and my life.* The prayer about this is for discernment, to rightly define what to let in and what to keep out. In addition to that discernment, clear action is needed, as not just anything needs to be allowed access. What comes in, and what does not, can either strengthen or weaken the health of my house and life.

In the midst of complicated days, these were simple words of clear wisdom, very valuable — for me, and for each of us.

Prayer points about this:

1. Prayer over the foundation of our homes and families, and over our own lives.

2. Prayer over the moat — declaring the surround of the blood of Jesus.

3. Prayer for the drawbridge — for discernment, wisdom on what to let in, and what to keep out.

4. Asking God's help to put this into action. Let's build this!

KEY #36 – Build on Jesus' life-surround and clear discernment.

37
Clutter

I was on a prayer drive along the Inlet one day in early spring. And I saw an incoming tide, quite a high tide. I also saw what looked like TONS of dirty chunks of ice all along the Inlet sides; in some areas, it was wide enough to block the flow of incoming water. Chunks — frozen — with no place to go, and blocking the progress of water coming in.

Here's what came to mind as I saw that: *"CLEAR the CLUTTER."* Clear anything that blocks the flow of New.

The direction I felt was to clear both outer and inner clutter — the extraneous, the unneeded, stuff that doesn't fit for now. Things that used to have a use, but don't any longer.

Outwardly, I know it well — there's lots of clutter at my house! Closets, corners, edges, take your pick — in my house, car, and purse. Clutter. And right now, in the springtime, I want to attack all of it and clear it. I get to some areas, and I clear some — but there are LOTS of areas that I do not.

What about inner clutter? That's harder to spot, because it fits in with the comfortable and familiar. Even familiar patterns that are no longer fitting or useful.

"Oh Father, help! Point out the clutter on the inside: that which is hard to see, that which carries its own cover — the cover that matches my blinders."

"Yes, Father, let's clear these things, so I can welcome the flow of what You are bringing in, the springtime things that are new."

I know that true springtime, fresh and clear, will be worth it.

Isaiah 43:16a, 18 —

> "Thus says the Lord, who makes a way in the sea, a path in the mighty waters… 'Remember not the former things, nor consider the things of old. Behold, I am doing a new thing; now it springs forth, do you not perceive it? I will make a way in the wilderness and rivers in the desert'…"

Clearing — It's worth the effort.

Clearing makes room for new days, and fresh springtime.

KEY #37 – *Clear space for new days!*

38
Beauty

– AUGUST 2022 –

In a book about overcoming and about enduring strength, the topic of beauty might seem too basic. I mean, simple beauty — how important could that be? Except that God is Creator, and what He makes has His fingerprints on it. Maybe simple is actually powerful.

Beauty — there's just something indefinably special about it. Beauty lifts our eyes from the everyday and ordinary to see something splendid.

A glimpse that brings hope.

That little flower peeking up through the crack in the pavement. The fresh color of a rainbow across the sky. The texture of a homespun weaving.

Little things. But somehow, they foster encouragement. The non-mundane. The glimpse of the Creator. Beauty — God created. And He said it was good.

These reminder scriptures come to mind:

Psalm 50:2: *"Out of Zion* (place of His presence) *the perfection of beauty, God shines forth."*

And Psalm 96:6: *"Splendor and majesty are before him; strength and beauty are in his sanctuary."*

His Presence, the very definition of beauty.

I think of stories about people who were in dire circumstances; they saw one little thing of beauty, like a tiny singular flower. And their spirits were lifted, a spark of hope was kindled. As they went on from that moment, they didn't give up, but continued in hope.

Hope — that's a precious commodity when times are hard. And beauty can bring that moment, that glimpse of Creator God. The glimpse that lifts our hearts and brings encouragement to carry on.

Oh Father, help us to stop and look, and actually see. See the beauty in what You've created, and beauty in each other, beauty all around. Open our eyes, Father, to see what You show us!

KEY #38 – *Simply powerful.*
Lift our eyes to see His handiwork!

39
The God of Rainbows and Light Sabers

– AUGUST 2022 –

Tonight, I saw a rainbow. Mike and I were leisurely riding together on our Harley, just enjoying the beautiful evening, taking in the Anchorage hillside views. What a treat! We stopped and took photos.

And although unseen by us in that sunny moment, there in the photo that Mike took of me was a beautiful, bright rainbow, right beside me in the snapshot. What a great glimpse! The symbol of God's promise of covenant with us.

Wow, Lord! Thank You for the rainbow in that photo!

It reminds me of an evening several years ago, a December date night in downtown Anchorage. Like tonight, Mike took a photo of me. That time, in the photo my hand held what appeared to be a "light saber!" When I saw the photo I thought, "Whoa! Don't mess with that girl!"

Thank You, Father, for Your Presence; and I love it that sometimes, You give a wonderful surprise, a glimpse of You being there.

Glimpses of Your Presence — I'm reminded anew of my "life verse," Psalm 27:4:

> "One thing have I asked of the Lord, that will I seek after: that I may dwell in the house of the Lord all the days of my life, to gaze upon the beauty of the Lord and to inquire in his temple."

ONE THING — clear, singular focus. It's my heart's aim. Dwelling with Him, in interactive relationship. ALL my days — not only young days, but continuing. And He shows up! Showing us glimpses of Him being there — because we're looking!

So, in these days and onward, I believe He's inviting us to actively look for His glimpses! To not miss them, but to be willing to embrace a sense of wonder, willing to be a child, a dear one, who believes. The God of rainbows and light sabers — *He invites us to come along with Him on an adventure, and look for His clues.*

He's true, He's real, and His invite is open!

KEY #39 – *Keep a sense of wonder. Be willing to see the glimpses of His presence!*

40
Don't Miss Dessert

– SPRING OF 2023 –

How valuable do you think it is, to know that Jesus loves and rewards our keeping high value on His covenant? Both in marriage and in relationship with Him. Valuing covenant may help us to "stay the course" through the years, in either case. Maybe that's why this long-ago scene came to mind recently:

Mike and I were on a winter vacay Out from Alaska. It was in the early 2000's, and we had been married about 35 years. We were driving through the California desert toward Lake Havasu, Arizona, looking forward to a few weeks there in Warmland. We were approaching that oasis in the desert when I heard this word to my heart: *"Don't miss dessert."*

"What??"

The same phrase repeated, *"Don't miss dessert. Don't miss it."*

"What do you mean, Lord?"

These words and a picture followed. The picture was of *marriage being like a fine feast,* a beautiful dinner with several courses. I saw the succession of courses. There was the "salad course" time, the early years. Often slimmer, and with thinner budget. A picture of a simpler and more basic time.

Then I saw the "main course," the years of greatest busyness, with more time spent in jobs or career paths, often more complex with activities, and school schedules of any children. So busy that the greatest challenge of this part could be time for each other.

And then the "dessert course," the later years, often calmer, with a slower pace and more relaxed time.

But His voice continued, *"Many miss dessert."*

I asked, *"Why, Lord? Who would want to miss dessert??"* (Said this dessert-loving girl!)

In a sad tone, He said, *"Some don't live long enough. And some don't stay married long enough. And some* (in the saddest tone of all)... *some don't believe for it. They don't believe there is more."*

Again, I thought, WHO would want to miss dessert??

A verse came to mind, Proverbs 29:18:

> *"Where there is no prophetic vision, the people cast off restraint..."* [they lose their way]

Without a vision, we can forget how much God loves us, we can forget that He has MORE up ahead. More, because He always has plans, and His plans are always good!

There were further thoughts on this theme during that oasis time — more detail in the dinner and dessert picture. And big emphasis on how much God loves and blesses keeping covenant. And that He has much more for us.

I realize too that there are variations on this simple picture of courses. Many who marry with children already in the family, marry right into the main course. Brave souls! Just one variation of the many that are possible.

But still, some thoughts about God's promise of blessing covenant: making it through the most intense time, the main course years, can be helped by knowing there's the promise of dessert! There are also wonderful things all along the way, because of God giving beautiful surprises all through the years. And yet, there is more. Beautifully more!

I believe He also emphasized the "dessert" promise for the later years because it counters a prevailing view in our culture: that after a certain number of years, there's decline and boring dullness, down to nothingness. A false view, and certainly NOT God's view. It's a reason to speak (and in my case, write) about this fresh vision.

Dessert — just picture the most outrageously delicious dessert! And enjoyed in an atmosphere of ease, not rushing but savoring the deliciousness. The phrases that came to me were, *"savor this time,"* and *"sip the sweet together."* Like a fine wine, God saves the best for last. (See John 2:10.)

And He reminded me, *"Don't miss it."*

I have remembered this in the many years since that moment of hearing this word as we drove across the desert to the beauty of an oasis. A reminder to enjoy, and to enjoy it together. We've been through plenty of hardships since that time: a couple more moves, the loss of my parents and other family and friends; been through Mike's cancer and treatment months, one church implosion and a pandemic. But the phrase and the promise has remained, *"Don't. Miss. Dessert."*

Why? Because our Father God IS that good!

* * *

**IMPORTANT NOTE! It's crucial for us to realize that this message is not only about marriage. It's a huge message to each of us, whether married or not, about our covenant with God. We who have received Jesus are called the Bride of Christ. So, our life in Him has covenant promises. And the courses of a great feast. Same beautiful picture!

He says in Psalm 34:8, *"Taste and see that the Lord is good."* And as I noted earlier — like a fine wine, God saves the best for last.

The delicious dessert of His Presence grows through the years, and extends past this life into eternity. It's not all for later — it's for experiencing in the Now, AND continuing into the forever zone.

Talk about a Great Dessert!

His covenant promises.

A fresh vision of this strengthens us through all the stuff, all the Now.

***KEY #40** – Savor dessert and the strength of fresh vision!*

41
World Book Dreams

– 2023 –

I am increasingly realizing the value of dreams, and of seeing where God has fulfilled dreams that He gave. Recognizing them gives increased vision and direction as well as gratitude to our days — such a key to persevering in faith. This scene from long ago was a recent reminder of a dream in my heart:

Sitting in the cozy corner, right by the couch. Poring over the pages, excitedly reading. What a vivid memory.

I was about 8 years old, and my family and I lived in a compact 2-bedroom house in our town of Fargo, North Dakota. I loved this house, especially the cheery kitchen, filled with the aromas of my mom's soups and breads. Other parts of our closeknit family lived nearby. My world was neatly framed by school and church and family, all within a couple miles' radius. That radius also included the small market down the block, a favorite place I rode my bike to, where I was well known to the mom & pop owners. The people in my town were nearly all

Caucasian, many Scandinavian like me. This was my world, a very-vanilla, pleasant place.

And yet, there's that distinct scene I recall from that time. It's 8-year-old me, sitting in the corner of our living room, reading the encyclopedia. I was so excited — we'd just bought these, a set highly valued for families at that time. Ours was World Book Encyclopedia — a regal blue, with the smell of fresh printing. In my cozy corner, I pored over the narratives and especially the pictures, for hours on end. My main interests: distant lands, other cultures, distinctly different people. I was so intrigued. I'd been to Minnesota lake cottages, and once we even drove to California, but that was it. I dreamed of much more.

Fast forward 10+ years, and I married "the boy down the block," who had also only lived in Fargo. The expectation was that we'd remain. But God...

My husband joined the Army, and we left Fargo to move to many assignments, where we met people from so many backgrounds. God and Army kept moving us, nearly always cross-country. We saw such varied landscapes, so many glimpses of great beauty. And diverse people groups, multiple backgrounds and accents and styles. Early in this journey we came into personal faith in Jesus, and through the years got to know many parts of the diverse body of Christ.

And then, Alaska — as you know by now, it was bigger and wider than I'd ever seen. My heart was similarly stretched with the setting. Our beloved adopted home ever since. Through the years, my extended family grew to include people from Peru and India and Africa, and our dear friends from Russia and Ukraine, Bolivia and Mexico. And more.

The dream — and an 8-year-old girl who excitedly held the World Book in her hands, and dreamed of seeing a wider world than she knew. *Oh God, Oh Father, You knew… it was Your dream You placed in my young heart. One that You were going to fulfill.*

Dreams — from God, fulfilled by God. I love His surprises! Do you have dreams? A wonderful challenge is to ask God to show you His dream for you. As you open your hands and your heart, He can show you more, and bring His plan. His plans are beautiful.

Psalms 37:23 (NLT): *The Lord directs the steps of the godly. He delights in every detail of their lives.*

KEY #41 – Ask God about HIS dreams — for you!

42
Crossroads

– 2023 –

Recently, I've been reminded of a scene from decades back, one that is pertinent now. A time not long after the encounter mentioned in this book's Prelude, the original "Parable of the Fly:"

The scene: So long ago. Mike and I and our two young sons were on a highway, heading east — nearing a crossroads, the offramp near Benson, Arizona. The offramp would lead to the familiar route: the road to Sierra Vista, a place I knew well.

Life had been good there. The first house we owned; a place of fresh faith, nurtured in a warm Christian community. Our home, the setting of that parable. The home we had loved.

But now, we were moving — going north, and north, and north; it seemed to the ends of the earth. Into the unknown. To a destination where we'd never lived. A place that would actually turn out very well. But at that moment, the decision moment, it was hard. The decision: continue forward and into the unknown future, or return to the familiar.

The clear voice in my heart at that moment said:

> *"You could go back. You could choose that. You did love it there. Know why? It was My presence there with you. Plenty of people hated it there — got divorced there, were miserable there. But you loved it. It was because of My presence, My blessing.*
>
> *So, you could go back — but My blessing, for you, would not be there. Because We are moving. Like the cloud, I am going forward, this way —> My presence, this way… ARE YOU WITH ME??"*

Oh, I got it, and I said through my tears, *"Yes, I am with You."* And I moved forward — to Alaska, a place that as you've read, turned out VERY well, and that we adopted as our always home.

Oh, but that decision moment — it was so hard, so pivotal.

* * *

That long-ago scene has come vividly to mind recently, along with the reminder that we who are in the journey with Jesus in our lives, are at a similar moment. Decision point. Going forward, or back to the familiar? In our recent years, so many things for all of us have been shaken up. Things like our accustomed ways of doing life. Our mindset.

As we've already spoken of here, we had our comfortable same-same world interrupted with pandemic and ensuing upset — so many parts of our lives were changed and rearranged. "Usual" things were reassessed and some discarded. Gathering especially took on different modes and ways.

The shaking. Part of moving toward a *"new wineskin,"* new ways of thinking and acting, new ways of gathering and of being "the church," the hands and feet of Jesus.

"New wineskin," after all, is to hold new wine. *New fresh life.* All the shaking of these years — shaking out forms and patterns, and re-examining others. Some aspects have been highlighted in importance, like family time; valuing even more greatly those relationships and other vital connections with intentional time together. Emphasizing what is real and actually anchoring. And what is not.

And now, there is more opportunity to return to comfortable patterns. To return to same-same. But will we forget what He's been doing? *Like a car on cruise control that encounters an interruption and slows down, will we now just push the "resume" button like nothing important happened?*

Decision point, an opportunity to join Him in the forward momentum, going somewhere wonderful. Yes, in the middle of shaking, we ARE going somewhere wonderful! He has shown the places of real connection, the unchanging anchoring points. That's part of the new as well. Anchoring what is genuinely valuable. What is Him — and what is just fluff and filler and outdated patterns.

And along the way, we're to not give up meeting together, as are certainly the current ways of many. (Hebrews 10:25) But there's importance in getting together in fresh, real, trimmed-up ways. Not just "programs for programs' sake," but following His lead.

So, I'm thankful for this current reminder to reaffirm that long ago *"yes."*

I'm saying yes, moving forward. Not going back. I'm here for the journey. Are you too?

Jesus is our Journey-Leader — with Him, the adventure will be grand!

KEY #42 – *Choose to keep moving forward, led by His presence.*

CONCLUSION

The central question of this book: *"How will we stand when times are tough? How will we make it through?"* And we can add by now in this reading, how do we *not only survive, but thrive?*

Through the treasure hunt of all the vignettes collected here, we have seen so many keys:

Keeping a single focus on God — facing fears — knowing who we are in Christ — having interactive relationship with Father — staying out of the muck — forgiving ourselves and others — embracing His changes — trusting His faithfulness — dancing in step with Him — trusting the Gardener, allowing His process — seeing His weaving, what He is bringing together — BEING Agent 99 — realizing that peace is a Person — just a few of many huge truths!

Inviting His deep-down core healing — recognizing and trusting His guardianship, His provision — walking in joy — keeping a sense of wonder — looking for His glimpses — welcoming His refreshing — worshiping Him — drinking in of His beauty — and not missing dessert! And keeping on, moving forward, in His presence.

Keys of vibrant fresh life, strength that WILL make it through ANYTHING!

We've looked at those many parts of the answer. But the biggest key of all was pointed out back at the beginning, in the Prelude of this book, in the original *"Parable of the Fly."*

Remember that? As the fly lay dead on the floor, the words I heard:

> *"That's who will fall — the 'fat and sassy ones,' boastful and proud; the ones who say, 'I'll never fall.' They will fall easily, and unexpectedly. But the young ones — they will know that they need help and will cry out to Me — and I will watch over them, so they will be fine. It's the other ones who will fall."*

"…the fat and sassy ones, boastful and proud…" There's a warning that my heart has been hearing. It's about pride — being cocky, know-it-all, abrasive, "strutting." A phrase I keep hearing is this: *"Do not strut."*

Like the fly — it was an ordinary fly. But so puffed up that it looked like a huge bee. Nevertheless, it fell like it was just air, with no substance. Like it was… nothing.

The biggest key to standing is… humility.

Knowing that we need Him. Not a lack of confidence — it is knowing who we are, His daughters, His sons, His beloved. But knowing that it's in Him. He is God. Our Father AND our King.

True humility: knowing it's in Him we stand.

My prayer is for each of us to see this clearly, and to truly walk in this.

Father, it's in YOU that we are going to make it. In You, we will flourish, in You we will have strength in the middle of anything. In You we will thrive.

We give ourselves to You. Our dear Father, it's YOU.

In Jesus' wonderful name we pray. Amen.

It's in **HIM.**
JESUS *is THE Key.*

DEAR READER

Thank you for reading through this collection of vignettes, and seeing so many keys!

I encourage you to keep these keys, pray through the ideas they highlight, and have your own key collection!

As I've now looked through all these writings that span so many years, I realize that God has taken me on the journey of a lifetime.

But that journey is not exclusive. I believe that He invites you too, to travel with Him, the Faithful One.

I extend this same invitation to you. Join in on the journey. You won't regret it.

God bless you, dear traveler!

Barbara Rawalt

For questions, comments, or testimonies — you can contact me on FB or Instagram, or email at *parableofthefly@gmail.com.*

APPENDIX:
KEYS TO TRUE STRENGTH

*From Prelude: The Way Forward — Be a "young one" on an adventure.
1. Keep singular focus and clear aim.
2. Treasure what He treasures. Listen.
3. Face the fears. Look for the gifts.
4. Look for the tools God gives.
5. Realize God-in-us makes a whole world of difference.
6. Keep interacting with Him, in relationship that is alive!
7. Live at the River, His separate ecosystem.
8. In mucky days, watch our steps!
9. Counter the culture. Pray. Strengthen on the inside.
10. Wear this: His steady love and faithfulness.

* * *

11. Wounds happen. Take time for healing in His presence.
12. Practice "…the unforced rhythms of grace."
13. Dance freely and celebrate His grace!
14. Prep for change. Trust Him in "Wow, what a ride!"
15. Look for the signposts. Notice and honor what He has done.
16. Hear our name: Beloved. We are His field, His vineyard.
17. Trust the most caring Gardener ever.
18. Use our time well. Lean in and listen.
19. Small can be big. Dial-down and see the new view.
20. Be a counter-cultural HOPE-carrier! Invest in lemon-yellow!
21. Trimming can be good. Welcome the trim and the new "digs."

22. God is bigger than our boxes. It's worth it to go with Him.
23. Remember, peace is a Person, anywhere He leads.
24. Release our voices in worship, and shift the atmosphere!
25. Live ready to reach out. Connect with trustworthy partners.
26. Align with the King and counter chaos. Be ON Team 99!
27. Especially for givers, there's a time to receive.
28. See His view, and discern the contrasts.
29. Feed on real timeless truth! Remember Who is really ruling.

* * *

30. Storm-proofing. Rock is solid! Sturdy in adversity.
31. Use the turnkey and let His strong peace rule.
32. Don't overlook simple. Breathers are vital for endurance.
33. Simply receive from the Master Healer.
34. Receive His bright promises! KNOW His guardianship and provision.
35. Remember that Joy is a weapon — it's our strength!
36. Build on Jesus' life-surround and clear discernment.
37. Clear space for new days!
38. Simply powerful. Lift our eyes to see His handiwork!
39. Keep a sense of wonder. Be willing to see the glimpses of His presence!
40. Savor dessert and the strength of fresh vision!
41. Ask God about HIS dreams — for you!
42. Choose to keep moving forward, led by His presence.

*And from Conclusion: It's in HIM. JESUS is THE Key.

*"...keeping our eyes on Jesus, the champion
who initiates and perfects our faith."*
Hebrews 12:2a (NLT)

ABOUT THE AUTHOR

Barbara Rawalt is an intercessor, encourager, and journal-keeper. An introvert with extrovert tendencies! Raised in a closeknit family in a Midwest small town, she later lived in several places across the US during her husband's military career. Her writing has been influenced by that rich variety of locales and cultures.

Her passion is connecting across generations and cultures, conveying the fresh reality of life in Jesus. Word pictures are often part of that sharing, inviting the reader into her story.

Barbara loves viewing nature on prayer drives along Cook Inlet near her home, meeting with friends over coffee, and enjoying sunset motorcycle rides with her husband Mike. They and their family, including many grandchildren, live in Anchorage, Alaska.

This is Barbara's first book.